## Early praise for *Functional Programming with Elixir*

Learning to program in a functional style requires one to think differently. When learning a new way of thinking, you cannot rush it. I invite you to read the book slowly and digest the material thoroughly. The essence of functional programming is clearly laid out in this book and Elixir is a good language to use for exploring this style of programming.

➤ **Kim Shrier**
Independent Software Developer, Shrier and Deihl

Some years ago it became apparent to me that functional and concurrent programming is the standard that discriminates talented programmers from everyone else. Elixir's a modern functional language with the characteristic aptitude for crafting concurrent code. This is a great resource on Elixir with substantial exercises and encourages the adoption of the functional mindset.

➤ **Nigel Lowry**
Company Director and Principal Consultant, Lemmata

This is a great book for developers looking to join the world of functional programming. The author has done a great job at teaching both the functional paradigm and the Elixir programming language in a fun and engaging way.

➤ **Carlos Souza**
Software Developer, Pluralsight

# Learn Functional Programming with Elixir
## New Foundations for a New World

Ulisses Almeida

The Pragmatic Bookshelf

Raleigh, North Carolina

Many of the designations used by manufacturers and sellers to distinguish their products are claimed as trademarks. Where those designations appear in this book, and The Pragmatic Programmers, LLC was aware of a trademark claim, the designations have been printed in initial capital letters or in all capitals. The Pragmatic Starter Kit, The Pragmatic Programmer, Pragmatic Programming, Pragmatic Bookshelf, PragProg and the linking *g* device are trademarks of The Pragmatic Programmers, LLC.

Every precaution was taken in the preparation of this book. However, the publisher assumes no responsibility for errors or omissions, or for damages that may result from the use of information (including program listings) contained herein.

Our Pragmatic books, screencasts, and audio books can help you and your team create better software and have more fun. Visit us at *https://pragprog.com*.

The team that produced this book includes:

Publisher: Andy Hunt
VP of Operations: Janet Furlow
Managing Editor: Brian MacDonald
Supervising Editor: Jacquelyn Carter
Series editor: Bruce A. Tate
Copy Editor: Candace Cunningham, Nicole Abramowitz
Indexing: Potomac Indexing, LLC
Layout: Gilson Graphics

For sales, volume licensing, and support, please contact *support@pragprog.com*.

For international rights, please contact *rights@pragprog.com*.

ISBN-13: 978-1-68050-245-9

Book version: P1.0—February 2018

# Contents

# Acknowledgments

When it is your first time writing a book, it's a great challenge. But when English isn't your native language, it's a challenge on a whole new level. I did it, but I wasn't alone. This book has reached this level of quality with the help of several amazing and kind people. I would like to highlight my editor, Jackie Carter. Her contribution is what makes the release of this book possible. Her experience and knowledge guided me in the right direction with patience and humor. We faced tough decisions, rewrites, and corrections, and she was always there to help and keep me motivated. I'm really grateful to have worked with her.

Bruce Tate, the series editor, took the first technical look at the book early in the writing process. His experience was invaluable to me. He helped me transform introductions from boring to engaging, and helped me prioritize the essential and useful functional programming techniques.

The Elixir core members Andrea Leopardi and James Fish provided great technical advice throughout the writing of this book. Our technical reviewers did superb work in catching broken code and pointing out concepts that needed more clarity: thank you to Bernardo Araujo, Stéfanni Brasil, João Britto, Thiago Colucci, Mark Goody, Gábor László Hajba, Maurice Kelly, Nigel Lowry, Max Pleaner, Juan Ignacio Rizza, Kim Shrier, Carlos Souza, Elomar Souza, and Richard Thai. Thank you also to our beta reviewers who did an excellent job in reporting issues, especially Luciano Ramalho, who shared his experience by providing excellent insights for the first examples of this book.

Thank you to Susannah Davidson Pfalzer for the excellent onboarding to The Pragmatic Bookshelf, and for the early tips on how to write a great book; Candace Cunningham, our copyeditor, who helped make the text fluid and enjoyable to read; Janet Furlow, who helped with production details and extractions; and Katharine Dvorak, who did an amazing job in guiding the book through the final steps. She was always ready to answer any questions and help me with book promotion.

Thank you to Hugo Baraúna from Plataformatec and Adriano Almeida from Casa do Código for introducing me to The Pragmatic Bookshelf; and to my coworkers from Plataformatec, who helped keep me motivated, especially João Britto and José Valim, who always helped me answer hard questions about Elixir.

Finally, I want to thank my family—Ana Guerra, Sandra Regina, and Thamiris Herrera—and friends for helping me focus on this project and filling me with good energy. Thanks to them, I was able to keep my motivation to work hard and finish the book.

# Introduction

As a child, I played many games that were very similar—games like Super Mario Bros., Donkey Kong, The Lion King, and Aladdin. I could switch between them without much work; the learning ramp-up was quick. They all shared the same core mechanics: you move straight to the right, jump on platforms, and avoid being hit by enemies. They were all 2D platform games.

Switching between programming languages is similar. In my work, I have needed to switch between Ruby, JavaScript, and CoffeeScript, and between Java, Python, and Objective-C. It wasn't too painful to do. All these languages are very different, but in some ways they are similar. I could use object-oriented programming with all of them. When I learned how to create objects and methods, all the dots started to connect and the languages became familiar quickly.

After playing 2D platform games, I switched to fighting games. They were still games. They were still 2D. However, the challenges and mechanics were completely different. Instead of going straight to the right and jumping the obstacles, I needed to punch and kick the enemies in a limited space. I needed to think differently to master this type of game.

That's how I felt when I switched to functional programming. Where were my objects and methods? I made the mistake of applying the concepts that I was used to in a paradigm where they aren't necessary. I was messing up the codebase. I needed to change my thinking. I couldn't program like I had before.

Switching to a new paradigm is very different from simply switching between languages. You need to think differently, or you'll get in trouble.

I invite you to reset your mind before learning functional programming. After reading this book you'll see your old code from a very different perspective. The best part is that most of today's main languages support some functional concepts. Even if you can't switch to Elixir today, you'll be able to apply useful functional concepts in your daily language.

## Is This Book for You?

This book is tailored for beginners in functional programming and Elixir. I expect you have some experience in building simple algorithms, debugging errors, and running commands in a terminal, and that you have at least an entry-level knowledge of software development. Any experience in other languages will help you out. You don't need to be an expert because we'll start from scratch.

If you're an object-oriented programmer ready to take the next step, or a college student graduating and looking for a language to work with, this book is for you. If you've tried to program in Elixir before and had a hard time because of the functional programming concepts, this book will give you the knowledge that you need to become a future expert. If you're already an Elixir or functional programming expert, you may find some valuable tips here, but this book probably isn't for you.

## What's in This Book?

You'll find a beginner's guide to functional programming concepts and an introduction to Elixir. The book is divided into seven chapters:

Chapter 1, *Thinking Functionally*, on page 1, introduces the main concepts of functional programming that will persist throughout the book. You'll learn why functional concepts matter and help you create better software.

In Chapter 2, *Working with Variables and Functions*, on page 11, you'll start learning Elixir from scratch, from simple expressions to modules. We'll explore the base building blocks of a functional program: *functions*. Anonymous and named functions are introduced here.

Then, in Chapter 3, *Using Pattern Matching to Control the Program Flow*, on page 33, you'll learn how to create conditional code with functions. Pattern matching plays the central role.

Repetition is a fundamental task in any programming language. In Chapter 4, *Diving into Recursion*, on page 59, you'll learn the functional way: recursive functions.

In Chapter 5, *Using Higher-Order Functions*, on page 81, we'll explore how to create better functions that hide complex code. We'll cover how to create functions that can receive or return functions; you'll learn higher-order functions.

Chapter 6, *Designing Your Elixir Applications*, on page 105, is about creating a larger application and organizing it. We'll explore how to model data, create contracts, and achieve polymorphism using Elixir.

Finally, in Chapter 7, *Handling Impure Functions*, on page 139, we'll look at the concept that finishes this journey: how to work with impure functions. We'll explore the pros and cons of four strategies: conditional code, exception handling, monads, and Elixir's with.

At the end of the book you'll find two appendixes. In Appendix 1, *Adding Rooms to the Game*, on page 161, you'll find extra challenges for the game you developed in Chapter 6, *Designing Your Elixir Applications*, on page 105. In Appendix 2, *Answers to Exercises*, on page 165, you'll find the answers for the exercises.

## Using Elixir

Elixir is a functional programming language that runs in the Erlang VM, a powerful environment to run distributed systems. I've chosen Elixir for this book because of its fun syntax, the vibrant community, and the production-ready tooling. Elixir syntax lets you focus on what's important while learning functional programming.

### Installing Elixir

Elixir needs Erlang to run; the Elixir installer installs Erlang for you. There's not a lot to say about the Elixir install steps if you follow the official Elixir installation guide.[1] It covers everything you need to know to install Elixir in each of the main operating systems. Read the guide, and be sure to install the latest Elixir version (1.6.0 or newer) so you can follow along with the examples in the book.

### Running the Code

For some examples, you'll need to write commands in your terminal. They will look like this:

```
$ elixir -v
Erlang/OTP 20 [erts-9.2] [source] [64-bit] [smp:4:4] [ds:4:4:10]
[async-threads:10] [hipe] [kernel-poll:false]

Elixir 1.6.0 (compiled with OTP 19)
```

The command elixir -v goes after the $ sign. Press Enter after typing the command to see the result. If you try that command, the result will show you that you have Elixir 1.6.0 installed (or a newer version).

---

1. https://elixir-lang.org/install.html

We'll also work with some Elixir tools that use the terminal, especially in Chapter 6, *Designing Your Elixir Applications*, on page 105. The main tool we'll use in many examples is Elixir's interactive shell, IEx. Try it:

```
$ iex
Erlang/OTP 20 [erts-9.2] [source] [64-bit] [smp:4:4] [ds:4:4:10]
[async-threads:10] [hipe] [kernel-poll:false]

Interactive Elixir (1.6.0) - press Ctrl+C to exit (type h() ENTER for help)
iex(1)>
```

You'll find this interactive shell very useful for quickly trying Elixir code and concepts, and gathering information to debug local and remote systems. Type the code that runs inside the IEx shell after the iex> prompt and press Enter to see the result. For example,

```
iex> IO.puts "Hello, World"
Hello, World
:ok
```

Inside IEx, you can press the Tab key to use autocomplete. You can exit by pressing Ctrl+C two times.

Moreover, some code will look like this:

```
introduction/hello_world.exs
IO.puts "Hello, World!"
```

The top line has the name of the file, with an exs (for script files) or ex (for compiled files) extension. You can execute the code inside of the files using the terminal, like this:

```
$ elixir hello_world.exs
Hello, World!
```

That's everything you need to know to use Elixir and run most of the examples in the book.

## Online Resources

You can find all the examples, a form to submit errata, and a community forum for this book on the Pragmatic Bookshelf website.[2] Additionally, you can get in touch with me and your fellow readers in the Elixir community forum for this book.[3]

---

2. https://pragprog.com/book/cdc-elixir/learn-functional-programming-with-elixir
3. https://elixirforum.com/t/learn-functional-programming-with-elixir-pragprog/5114

# CHAPTER 1

# Thinking Functionally

Our programming paradigm is changing. If that sentence doesn't scare you, let me try again. *The rules that govern typical everyday programming are changing.* That doesn't happen often. When it does, something important is going on.

You see, languages come and go. Many things might prompt a new language, such as a new problem (mobile development for Apple's Swift), a critical limitation (speed for C), or adoption across hardware platforms (portability for Java).

When programming paradigms change, something serious is out of balance.

## Why Functional?

A programming paradigm consists of the rules and design principles of building software. A paradigm change is serious business. It means something in how we're building software isn't meeting modern demands. We need to process multiple tasks and huge amounts of data quickly and reliably. The CPU isn't getting faster—we can't just write code and hope it will be faster with a new CPU launch. Instead, we have multiple cores or even machines to process stuff. We need to write code that takes advantage of concurrency and parallelism. Unfortunately, when you're working in imperative and object-oriented languages, it's hard to get it right. Let's take a closer look.

### The Limitations of Imperative Languages

Imperative languages have shared mutating values. This means that many parts of the program can reference the same value, and it can change. Mutating values can be dangerous for concurrency; you can easily introduce hard-to-detect bugs. For example, take a look at this script in Ruby:

```
list = [1, 2, 3, 4]
list.pop
# => 4
list.push(1)
# => [1, 2, 3, 1]

puts list.inspect
# => [1, 2, 3, 1]
```

In this chapter you'll see more code examples like the one above. Don't worry about the syntax or how the language works. The focus is on the concepts. Here, you can mutate the data by adding or removing elements. Now imagine multiple parts of an application running in parallel and having access to this value at the same time. What could happen if, in the middle of some operation, the value changes because of another process? It's hard to predict. It causes headaches for developers. That's why many features and libraries in these imperative languages offer mechanisms to help you lock and synchronize the changes. However, that's not the only way. Functional programming offers a better alternative.

## Moving to Functional Programming

Here's a quick overview: in the functional programming paradigm, functions are the basic building blocks, all values are immutable, and the code is declarative.

When you search online for "functional programming," a lot of unusual terms pop up. It's like it was made for mathematicians, not for programmers. It's no wonder some developers find functional programming languages have a high initial barrier to learning.

### From Lambda Calculus to Functional Programming

In this book you'll learn about anonymous functions, free and bound variables, and functions as first-class citizens. They come from the lambda calculus computation model, created by Alonzo Church in the 1930s.[a] This model is the smallest universal language that can simulate any real computation—that's *Turing complete*. If you see a programming language that has *lambdas*, you can be sure that Church's model has influenced it.

_____

a.    https://en.wikipedia.org/wiki/Lambda_calculus

Enter Elixir, a dynamic, functional language. The simple and pragmatic syntax of Elixir makes it an accessible programming language for everyone, even for those who haven't learned the functional paradigm. Elixir is a robust and production-ready language, and it lives in the Erlang ecosystem, which has existed for 30 years, delivering software with nine 9s reliability.[1]

With a functional language like Elixir, you'll make better use of your CPU multicores, writing shorter and more explicit code. When you apply the functional paradigm in a functional language, you write code that lives harmoniously with the language. But it doesn't come for free. You must understand and follow these core principles: *immutability*, *functions*, and *declarative code*. In this chapter, we'll examine these principles in detail and see how the functional foundation is better prepared for modern demands. Let's start with immutable data.

## Working with Immutable Data

Conventional languages use mutating shared values that require thread and lock mechanisms to work with concurrency and parallelism. In functional programming, all values you create in your program are *immutable*. By default, each function will have a stable value. That means we don't need lock mechanisms, which simplifies the parallel work. It changes everything about building software.

Look at this Elixir code:

```
list = [1, 2, 3, 4]
List.delete_at(list, -1)
# => [4]

list ++ [1]
# => [1, 2, 3, 4, 1]

IO.inspect list
# => [1, 2, 3, 4]
```

The value of list is immutable: no matter the operation we apply to it, it will generate new values. If the list is immutable and each operation has a safe value, the compiler can safely run these three lines in parallel without affecting the final result. We get the benefits of parallelism just by writing simple functions. It's a huge win. You may think, "All this transformation generating new values will be slow." It's not. Elixir has smart data structures that reuse values in memory, making every operation of transforming values very efficient.

Immutability is showing up more in conventional languages. Those languages usually provide the immutable mechanism by giving you an immutable-data-type alternative, or a method to turn a value immutable. For example, in Ruby you can create immutable values using the freeze method:

---

1. https://pragprog.com/articles/erlang

```
User = Struct.new(:name)
users = [User.new("Anna"), User.new("Billy")].freeze
# => [#<struct User name="Anna">, #<struct User name="Billy">]

users.push(User.new("James"))
# => can't modify frozen Array

users.first.name = "Karina"
puts users.inspect
# => [#<struct User name="Karina">, #<struct User name="Billy">]
```

In Ruby, when you freeze the array you can't add or remove items, but you still can modify the stored objects. I've seen many developers fall into a trap, thinking that by using freeze they were creating a safe immutable value.

It's easy to make mistakes when a language has mutability by default, and such mistakes are costly when you're dealing with concurrency. Although the conventional languages are adopting some functional programming concepts, they do not offer you the full advantage of a functional language ecosystem.

## Building Programs with Functions

In functional programming, functions are the primary tools for building a program. You can't create a useful program without writing or using functions. They receive data, complete some operation, and return a value. They are usually short and expressive.

We combine multiple little functions to create a larger program. The complexity of building a larger application is reduced when the functions have these properties:

- The values are immutable.
- The function's result is affected only by the function's arguments.
- The function doesn't generate effects beyond the value it returns.

Functions that have these properties are called *pure functions*. A simple example is a function that adds 2 to a given number:

```
add2 = fn (n) -> n + 2 end
add2.(2)
# => 4
```

This takes an input, processes it, and returns a value. This is the way most functions work. A few functions will be more complex—their results are unpredictable and they are known as *impure functions*. We'll look at them in Chapter 7, *Handling Impure Functions*, on page 139.

## Using Values Explicitly

Functional programming always passes the values explicitly between the functions, making clear to the developer what the inputs and outputs are. The conventional object-oriented languages use objects to store a state, providing methods for operating on that state. The object's state and methods are very attached to each other. If we change the object's state, the method invocation will result in a different value. For example, take a look at this Ruby code:

```ruby
class MySet
  attr_reader :items

  def initialize()
    @items = []
  end

  def push(item)
    items.push(item) unless items.include?(item)
  end
end

set = MySet.new
set.push("apple")

new_set = MySet.new
new_set.push("pie")

set.push("apple")
# => ["apple"]
new_set.push("apple")
# => ["pie", "apple"]
```

The MySet class doesn't allow repeated values. When we call set.push, the push method depends on the set object's internal state. As software evolves, the common tendency is for the object to accumulate more and more internal states. This generates a complex dependency between the methods and the states, which can be hard to debug and maintain. We need to be constantly disciplined about applying good practices.

Functional programming gives us an alternative. We can use the same MySet example in Elixir to do the same thing in a different way:

```elixir
defmodule MySet do
  defstruct items: []

  def push(set = %{items: items}, item) do
   if Enum.member?(items, item) do
    set
```

```
    else
      %{set | items: items ++ [item]}
    end
  end
end

set = %MySet{}
set = MySet.push(set, "apple")

new_set = %MySet{}
new_set = MySet.push(new_set, "pie")

IO.inspect MySet.push(set, "apple")
# => ["apple"]
IO.inspect MySet.push(new_set, "apple")
# => ["pie", "apple"]
```

You'll learn the details of how to create Elixir functions in Chapter 2, *Working with Variables and Functions*, on page 11, and structs in Chapter 6, *Designing Your Elixir Applications*, on page 105. The most important thing here is that the operations and data are not attached to each other. While in our Ruby example the operation must be called from a method that belongs to an object that contains data, in Elixir the operation exists on its own. The data must be explicitly sent to the MySet.push function. Every time we call the function, it generates a new data structure with updated values. Then we update the set variable to store the updated value and print it. The push function works with its arguments and returns a new value. Nothing more.

## Using Functions in Arguments

Functions are so interlaced with everything you do in functional programming that they can be used in the arguments and results of functions:

```
iex> Enum.map(["dogs", "cats", "flowers"], &String.upcase/1)
["DOGS", "CATS", "FLOWERS"]
```

Here we're executing a function called Enum.map and passing a list ("dogs", "cats", and "flowers") and a function called String.upcase. The Enum.map function knows how to apply String.upcase to each item in the list. The result is a new list with all words uppercased. Passing functions to other functions is a powerful and mind-blowing mechanism that we'll explore in detail in Chapter 5, *Using Higher-Order Functions*, on page 81. Functions are the star of the show in the functional paradigm.

## Transforming Values

Elixir's focus is on the data-transformation flow, and it has a special operator called pipe (|>) to combine multiple functions' calls and results. Let's say we want to write some code that takes text like "the dark tower" and transforms it into a title, "The Dark Tower". Instead of writing it like this:

```
def capitalize_words(title) do
  join_with_whitespace(
    capitalize_all(
      String.split(title)
    )
  )
end
```

you can write it like this:

```
def capitalize_words(title) do
  title
  |> String.split
  |> capitalize_all
  |> join_with_whitespace
end
```

Using the pipe operator, the result of each expression will be passed to the next function. (You'll learn more about it in *Pipelining Your Functions*, on page 89.) As you can see, this Elixir function is simple and easy to understand. You can almost read it as plain English. The function capitalize_words receives a title. The title will be split, transforming a list of words. The second transformation will be a list of capitalized words. The final transformation is a unique string with the words separated by whitespaces.

That's our focus in functional programming; every basic building block is a function. Those functions follow principles, such as immutability, that help us build functions that are easier to understand and that are better citizens in the concurrent world.

## Declaring Code

Imperative programming focuses on *how to solve a problem*, describing each step as actions. Functional programming, by contrast, is declarative. Declarative programming focuses on *what is necessary to solve a problem*, describing the data flow. Programming declaratively usually generates less code than programming imperatively. Less code means fewer things to write, more things done, and fewer bugs. Yay!

To see the difference between imperative and declarative, let's look at a simple example that transforms a list of strings into uppercase. The example will be in JavaScript using the imperative mindset:

```
var list = ["dogs", "hot dogs", "bananas"];
function upcase(list) {
  var newList = [];
  for (var i = 0; i < list.length; i++) {
    newList.push(list[i].toUpperCase());
  }
  return newList;
}

upcase(list);
// => ["DOGS", "HOT DOGS", "BANANAS"]
```

When you use the imperative mindset, you'll need *control flow* structures like for to navigate through each element of the list, incrementing the variable i one by one. Then, you need to push the new uppercased string in the newList variable. The code is verbose. The *what* that needs to be done is obfuscated by boilerplate actions and mutating values.

Let's experiment with the declarative version in Elixir. Declarative programming focuses on *what* is necessary, doing list navigations or repetition with recursive functions (more about this in Chapter 4, *Diving into Recursion*, on page 59):

```
defmodule StringList do
  def upcase([]), do: []
  def upcase([first | rest]), do: [String.upcase(first) | upcase(rest)]
end

StringList.upcase(["dogs", "hot dogs", "bananas"])
# => ["DOGS", "HOT DOGS", "BANANAS"]
```

The upcase result of an empty list is an empty list. When the list has items, the result is a new list where the first string is uppercased and the rest of the items are passed to the upcase function. We describe how the data must *be*, not the actions to generate the result. This way of expressing the code is possible thanks to *pattern matching*. You'll see the details about it in Chapter 3, *Using Pattern Matching to Control the Program Flow*, on page 33.

The procedure of transforming a list of strings to uppercase can be simplified using higher-order functions:

```
list = ["dogs", "hot dogs", "bananas"]
Enum.map(list, &String.upcase/1)
# => ["DOGS", "HOT DOGS", "BANANAS"]
```

This time we're saying that we want to map a list, applying the upcase transformation on each item. The map function builds a new collection using the result of the argument function. In this declarative version, we just say *what* needs to be done, and the *how* is abstracted for us. Today, Java, PHP, Ruby, Python, and many other languages are embracing the declarative style. It generates much simpler code. The important aspects of the task, the parts that matter, are explicit.

## Wrapping Up

Functional programming is a *programming paradigm*. A programming paradigm consists of the rules and design principles of building software; it's a way of thinking about a programming language. The functional paradigm focuses on building software using *pure functions* organized in a way that describes *what* software must do, not *how* it must do it. Now, with this in mind, you'll learn the programming foundations in detail, from scratch. You'll be introduced to Elixir syntax at the same time you learn functional concepts, at the right pace. Turn the page to start the journey.

# CHAPTER 2

# Working with Variables and Functions

Variables and functions are the fundamentals of any functional language, and Elixir is no different. It's important to have a solid understanding of how they work so you can be comfortable working with the various types of functions. In this chapter, we'll use Elixir to explore the basics and build a solid foundation for the upcoming advanced topics.

Our first topic will be values. In Elixir, valid values include strings, integers, floats, lists, maps, functions, and a few more. Yes, functions are values here, as you'll see later in the chapter. But first, let's take a look at how we can represent common values and their types.

## Representing Values

Values are anything that can represent data in Elixir. They are the number of cars purchased, the text in a blog post, the price of a game, the password text of a login. They are everything a program receives as input, computes, and generates as a result.

Open your IEx shell and type this:

```
iex> 10
10
```

You have typed a value. I know—this short snippet doesn't look very exciting, but when we think of everything that happens in the background to let us type a value like this, it's fascinating. When you see it, it's easy to guess that it represents a number. *Literals* represent values that humans can easily understand. Elixir does all the work to transform the literals into a format for machines. We only need to worry about typing the number we like, and Elixir will understand.

The number 10 that we used previously has a type—the integer type, which, of course, represents integers. Let's try a different kind of value. Try typing this in your IEx shell:

```
iex> "I don't like math"
"I don't like math"
```

Text surrounded by double quotes is a value of the String.t type. It's a literal, an abstraction that hides all the binary complexity for us. We can generate any text values by putting anything we want within double quotes. Try writing your messages using IEx. You can write the most popular program there is: "Hello, World".

The following table shows some types you'll find in Elixir, their uses, and some examples to try in your IEx shell:

| Type | Useful for | Examples |
|---|---|---|
| string | Text | "Hello, World!!!", "I like math" |
| integer | Integer numbers | 42, 101, 10_000, -35 |
| float | Real numbers | 10.8, 0.74678, -1.45 |
| boolean | Logical operations | true, false |
| atom | Identifiers | :ok, :error, :exit |
| tuple | Building collections of known sizes | {:ok, "Hello"}, {1, 2, 3} |
| list | Building collections of unknown sizes | [1, 2], ["a", "b"] |
| map | Looking up a value in a dictionary by key | %{id: 123, name: "Anna"}, %{12 => "User"} |
| nil | Representing absence of value | nil |

The atom type is a constant and its name is the value. Atoms are useful as identifiers. For example, the Boolean values (true and false) and nil are the atoms :true, :false, and :nil. Some types are more complex than others, but don't worry. We'll see them in more detail in the following chapters.

## Executing Code and Generating a Result

Elixir can generate a result for any expression. The process is similar to when you were in high school solving mathematical equations: to generate a result, you must add or multiply some numbers or change some Xs to Ys. We'll create expressions for the computer, and the computer will show us the result. The simplest expression is a value, like this:

```
iex> 42
42
```

The number 42 is an expression that evaluates to the value we typed. Let's try a different expression:

```
iex> 1 + 1
2
```

The number 1 is a value, and + is an operator. Operators compute values and generate a result. We can also combine multiple operators and values:

```
iex> (2 + 2) * 3
12
iex> 2 + 2 * 3
8
```

Each operator is executed in a particular order, which is called its *precedence*. For example, * has higher precedence than +. In an expression that has both operators, the * operator will be executed first. You can use parentheses to change the precedence, however. Expressions within parentheses are computed first. You can always check the operator's precedence in the Elixir official documentation.[1]

When we create invalid expressions, the computation will fail with an error message. Let's create an invalid expression and watch our shell complain:

```
iex> "Hello, World!" + 5
** (ArithmeticError) bad argument in arithmetic expression
    :erlang.+("Hello, World!", 5)
```

The arithmetic expression has an error because we can't add text and a number. The function behind the + operator expects number arguments, not strings. It's a common mistake. The execution will fail when we try to execute invalid code, and the error message will tell us what went wrong.

It's not always the case that an execution will fail when you use different arguments types. Some operations permit you to use compatible types, like this:

```
iex> 37 + 3.7
40.7
```

The sum of the integer 37 with the float 3.7 produced a float result of 40.7. The + operator works in this expression because both arguments are numbers. The number type in Elixir is the union of the integer and float types.

The table on page 14 shows some common Elixir operators. You can try the examples in IEx to get comfortable with them:

---

1.  https://hexdocs.pm/elixir/operators.html

| Operator | Useful for | Examples |
|---|---|---|
| + | Adding numbers | 10 + 5, 3.7 + 8.1 |
| - | Subtracting numbers | 10 - 25, 9.7 - 8.1 |
| / | Dividing numbers | 10 / 2, 0 / 10 |
| * | Multiplying numbers | 10 * 2, 0 * 10 |
| == | Checking when two values are equal | 1 == 1.0, 1 == 2 |
| != | Checking when two values are not equal | 1 != 1.0, 1 != 2 |
| < | Checking when the left value is less than the right one | 1 < 2, 2 < 1 |
| > | Checking when the left value is greater than the right one | 1 > 2, 2 > 1 |
| ++ | Concatenating two lists | [1, 2] ++ [3, 4] |
| <> | Concatenating two strings or binaries | "Hello, " <> "World" |

You don't need to memorize all these operators. You can always consult the Elixir official documentation for more operators and a detailed explanation of each.[2]

## Creating Logical Expressions

Logical expressions are often used to create conditions that control the program flow. In Elixir, we have two versions of the same logical operator—for example, for the logical operator *OR*, we have || and or. It can be confusing for newcomers. But don't worry; let's try the examples below and understand their differences:

The operators and, or, and not are made to work with Boolean values. Try this in your console:

```
iex> true and true
true
iex> true or false
true
iex> not true
false
iex> 1 and true
** (BadBooleanError) expected a Boolean on left side of "and", got: 1
iex> true and 1
1
```

---

2.  https://hexdocs.pm/elixir/Kernel.html

The left side of the operators and and or must be Boolean values, or an error will be raised. The operators &&, ||, and ! accept *truthy* and *falsy* values on their left side. Falsy values are false and nil, while truthy values are everything that isn't falsy. The value that will be returned depends on which operator we use. Try this in your IEx:

```
iex> nil && 1
nil
iex> true && "Hello, World!"
"Hello, World!"
iex> "Hello, Word!" && true
true
iex> nil || 1
1
iex> 1 || "Hello, World!"
1
iex> !true
false
iex> !false
true
iex> !nil
true
iex> !"Hello, World!"
false
```

The && operator is a kind of and that works with Booleans and values. It returns the second expression's value when the first is truthy; otherwise, it returns the first expression's value. The || is kind of or operator that works with Booleans and values. It returns the first truthy expression; otherwise, it returns the value of the last expression. These operators are useful for creating short expressions to return values such as cache_image || fresh_image. The ! operator returns true when the value is falsy, and returns false when it's truthy. It's useful to have the inverse boolean value of the truthy and falsy values.

## Binding Values in Variables

Variables are containers that hold values. My friend works with office facilities, and she organizes the office tools by putting them in boxes. She puts a label on boxes to help workers know what's inside without opening them. Variables are like that; you can't see what's inside without checking, but the variable's name can give you a hint. Let's create a variable using IEx:

```
iex> x = 42
42
iex> x
42
```

We've used the = operator to assign the name x to the value 42. This action of assigning a name to a value is called *binding*. We can bind new values and results of expressions in variables. Try it:

```
iex> x = 6
6
iex> x = 7
7
iex> x = 9 + 1
10
iex> x
10
```

The most interesting part of variables is that we can use them in our expressions instead of using the actual values. Here's an example:

```
iex> x = 5
iex> y = 8
iex> z = x * y
40
```

Take a look at the expression z = x * y and forget the previous steps. We can't see the values there, but we can guess that the x and y variables are numbers because we have the * operator. Variables encapsulate the values in programs; we don't need to work directly with values. We can create generic expressions with variables that can use any value to produce different results.

Remember the "box with a label" analogy? Yep, I discourage you from choosing names like x, y, and z for your variables, because they don't indicate what's inside the variables. Instead, choose names that reveal your intentions, knowing that the Elixir compiler doesn't care which name you choose. It will help your future self and your teammates when you're building and maintaining software. Take a look at the impact when we change the names of the variables:

```
total_cost = product_price * quantity
total_distance = average_velocity * total_time
total_damage_bonus = strength_score * magic_enchantment
```

With explicit names that clarify our intentions, our code now has meaning and purpose. From the expression z = x * y, we have opened up a world of possibilities by changing the variables' names.

You should use the Elixir community conventions when naming variables. The variables follow the *snake_case* format. That means your variable names should be lowercased and compound names should have the "_" (underline) separator. Here are some examples:

```
quantity = 10 # good
Quantity = 10 # match error
product_price = 15 # good
productPrice = 15 # works, but doesn't follow the Elixir style guide
```

You can't start a variable name with a capital letter. If you try, you'll get a match error. Names that start with a capital letter are used in modules. (You can learn more about Elixir naming conventions in the official documentation.[3])

### Naming Things Is Hard

To paraphrase the famous quote from Phil Karlton, the software architect of Netscape, one of the hardest parts of computer science is naming things. When we're programming, we usually borrow names from the real world, but we often need to work with things that have no parallel in reality. The impact of choosing a misleading name can be critical to software evolution, leading to developers making mistakes or taking too long to understand how the code works. It's beneficial to take your time and have a deep discussion with your teammates about choosing names that fit your intentions.

## Creating Anonymous Functions

You can think of functions as subprograms of your program. They receive an input, do some computation, and then return an output. The function body is where we write expressions to do a computation. The last expression value in the function body is the function's output. Functions are useful for reusing expressions. Let's start with a simple example in which we'll build messages to say hello to Ana, John, and the world. Try typing this in your IEx:

```
iex> "Hello, Mary!"
"Hello, Mary!"
iex> "Hello, John!"
"Hello, John!"
iex> "Hello, World!"
"Hello, World!"
```

If we want to say hello to Alice and Mike, we could copy and paste the message and replace the names. But instead we can create a function to make it easier to say hello to anything we want. First, we need to identify the things that change in the messages. In the preceding example, we can see that the only thing that changes is the name of the person or group we want to say hello to. We can write an expression that separates the name from the message. Try it:

---

3. https://hexdocs.pm/elixir/naming-conventions.html

```
iex> name = "Alice"
iex> "Hello, " <> name <> "!"
"Hello, Alice!"
```

We created the name variable that represents something that can change. Then we used the <> operator to join the strings with the name variable. To transform these expressions into a function, we transform the name variable in a parameter and the string concatenation in a function body. Let's take a look at the function-creation syntax. Try it in your IEx:

```
iex> hello = fn name -> "Hello, " <> name <> "!" end
iex> hello.("Ana")
"Hello, Ana!"
iex> hello.("John")
"Hello, John!"
iex> hello.("World")
"Hello, World!"
```

We created a function and bound it to a variable called hello. Then we invoked that using the *dot* operator and passing values inside the parentheses. We can invoke that function with different values in the argument. These types of functions are called *anonymous functions* in Elixir because they have no global name and must be bound to a variable to be reused. They are useful for creating functions on the fly. (They are also known as *lambdas* and are the only type of function in lambda calculus.)

Now let's go step by step through how we have defined the function:

1. The fn indicates the beginning of the function.

2. The name is the function's parameter. A function's parameters are internal function variables that force whoever is invoking the function to supply them with values. When calling a function we need to pass the values in the same order the parameters were defined.

3. We have the -> operator, which indicates the following expression will be the body of a function clause.

4. The function body is the expression "Hello, " <> name <> "!". The return value is the value of the last expression. In this example, there's only one expression, so the value of that expression will be returned.

5. The end marks the end of the function definition.

Elixir gives developers the power of redefining some of the language's basic functions and blocks by using metaprogramming. However, the fn and end combination is an Elixir special form. Special forms are basic building blocks that cannot be overridden by the developer. They'll always work in the same way no matter the framework or library that you're using in your application. You can see more details about special forms in Elixir's documentation.[4]

You can replace the <> operator with Elixir's expressive string-interpolation syntax:

```
iex> hello = fn name -> "Hello, #{name}!" end
iex> hello.("Ana")
"Hello, Ana!"
```

All the expressions inside of the brackets in the #{} code will be evaluated and coerced to a string. Here's an example:

```
iex> "1 + 1 = #{1+1}"
"1 + 1 = 2"
```

We commonly use anonymous functions for simple operations, and most of them will be on one line. But we can create them with multiple lines; just break the line after the -> operator:

```
iex> greet = fn name ->
...>    greetings = "Hello, #{name}"
...>    "#{greetings}! Enjoy your stay."
...> end
#Function<6.99386804/1 in :erl_eval.expr/5>
```

We can also create functions without arguments. We just need to omit them:

```
iex> one_plus_one = fn -> 1 + 1 end
iex> one_plus_one.()
2
```

We can create functions with multiple arguments, too, by separating them with commas:

```
iex> total_price = fn price, quantity -> price * quantity end
iex> total_price.(5, 6)
30
```

We've used commas to separate the parameters price and quantity. Elixir has a limit of 255 parameters in a function. That's enough for any application. However, it's good maintenance practice to keep the number of parameters below five. A higher number of parameters can be a good indication that you need a data structure—tuples, lists, structs, or maps—or you need to split your function into smaller ones.

---

4.    https://hexdocs.pm/elixir/Kernel.SpecialForms.html

## Functions as First-Class Citizens

The first time I read the term *first-class citizens*, I found it funny because I imagined a bunch of functions flying first class to Europe. But it means the opposite. When we say in programming that functions are first-class citizens, we mean that they are like any other value. It's an important feature that came from lambda calculus.

In Elixir, functions are values of type function. Let's build a function that expects a function:

```
iex> total_price = fn price, fee -> price + fee.(price) end
```

The function total_price receives two arguments; one is a number that will represent the price. The fee parameter expects a function. We'll call the given function, passing the price. The final result of the function is the result of the price plus the result of the fee function. Now, let's build some fee functions:

```
iex> flat_fee = fn price -> 5 end
iex> proportional_fee = fn price -> price * 0.12 end
```

Now we can try these functions all together:

```
iex> total_price.(1000, flat_fee)
1005
iex> total_price.(1000, proportional_fee)
1120.0
```

We first call the total_price function, passing the flat_fee, and then we call total_price another time, passing the proportional_fee function. In this example, we have passed a function in an argument like any other value. Functions are the actions in the program. Passing or returning actions in functions is what makes functional programming so different from imperative programming. We'll explore it more in Chapter 5, *Using Higher-Order Functions*, on page 81.

## Sharing Values Without Using Arguments

We can share values with functions using *closures*. A closure has access to variable values both inside and outside of the code block. In Elixir we can create an anonymous function and pass it a code block with the values of the variables that were defined outside of it. It's useful to be able to share values with functions when you can't control the functions' invocation, since you can't pass values to functions' parameters. You can't control function calls specially when you use functions that take other functions as arguments. For example, we can use Elixir's spawn to start a process and execute a function asynchronously. The spawn will invoke the given function asynchronously, and we can't pass arguments to it. One way to share values with that function is by taking advantage of the closure:

```
iex> message = "Hello, World!"
iex> say_hello = fn -> Process.sleep(1000); IO.puts(message) end
iex> spawn(say_hello)
"Hello, World!"
```

The function say_hello remembered the value of the message variable and printed the message on the console using IO.puts after one second using Process.sleep. We used the printing and sleeping commands on the same line using the semicolon. (The commands are named functions, and we'll see these types of functions in detail in the next section.) We have shared values with say_hello without using arguments. This is possible because closures remember all the free variables that were referenced in the lexical scope in which they were created. Free variables? Lexical scope? Let's see what these terms mean.

## Hey, We Have a Side Effect Here

In this section, we used a say_hello function. It calls IO.puts, displaying a message in our console session. The console and our program are different entities. When a function interacts with anything that is external, it's vulnerable to external problems. We say that function has side effects; it's impure. We'll discuss pure and impure functions in detail in Chapter 7, *Handling Impure Functions*, on page 139.

A scope is a part of a program—a code block, for example. The lexical scope is related to the visibility of the variables in the code where they were defined. When you use a variable in a function definition, the compiler will analyze your code reading upwards and will bind the variable to the closest definition. Everything defined before and outside of a function's scope is the upward scope. Try this example:

```
iex> answer = 42
iex> make_answer = fn -> other_answer = 88 + answer end
iex> make_answer.()
130
iex> other_answer
** (CompileError) iex:4: undefined function other_answer/0
iex> answer = 0
iex> make_answer.()
130
```

The function make_answer references the variable answer; the compiler will go to the upward scope and find the answer definition. When we try to call other_answer outside of the function's scope, the program will generate an error. That's because other_answer exists only inside of the make_answer function's scope, not outside of it. It's like a one-way mirror: the inner scope can *see* the variables outside, but not vice versa.

Also note the unaffected make_answer result after we assign a new value to answer. When we define a function referencing a variable outside of the function's scope, we bind the current value and it will be immutable. That's why when answer has a new value, it doesn't affect the make_answer function's result.

The following diagram illustrates how scopes work. The white box is the scope of the IEx shell, while the gray box is the scope of the anonymous function make_answer.

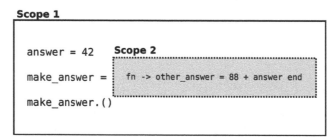

We can see each code block has his own space. The next diagram shows that each code block we create has a space that the code outside can't see into. But the code inside the space can see the variables defined outside and reference them. The gray shading color of the variable indicates that variable is not visible by the scope. The following diagram shows each scope's variable visibility:

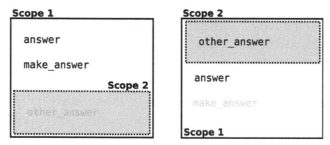

The outer scope can't see the variables defined inside of the anonymous function. The anonymous function can only see the variables defined before its own definition. That's why the anonymous function can't see the make_answer variable: it was defined after the function-creation expression.

With an understanding of how lexical scope works, we can now discuss free and bound variables. Inside of a function, a variable is bound when it is defined as a function's parameter or a local variable in a function's body; otherwise, it's free. Let's test the closure:

```
iex> product_price = 200
iex> quantity = 2
iex> calculate = fn quantity -> product_price * quantity end
iex> calculate.(4)
800
```

We've defined the variable quantity, but the function calculate has a parameter with the same name. This means the variable is bound, and its value will not be remembered. product_price is free, but it doesn't exist in the calculate parameter although it's referenced in the body. Therefore, the product_price value will be remembered no matter where the execution happens. The following diagram illustrates the scopes' definitions:

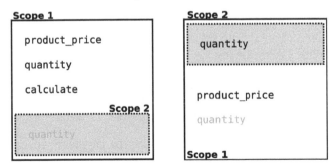

We can see the variables' visibility on each scope:

**Scope 1**

product_price

quantity

calculate

**Scope 2**

quantity

**Scope 2**

quantity

product_price

quantity

**Scope 1**

We can clearly see now that the quantity parameter defined in the inner scope has higher precedence than the variable with the same name defined in the outer scope. The outer variable quantity is shadowed by the quantity parameter in the calculate function. Variable shadowing isn't good practice because it creates confusion about the variable's value, generating code that is hard to understand. Avoid this! That's how closures work in Elixir: we can share values with functions without using arguments.

## Naming Functions

We've covered how to create anonymous functions, and they are awesome. We can bind them to variables, use them as a function's arguments, and return them in functions. However, having only anonymous functions can be annoying. If the codebase of a large application used only anonymous functions, it would be very complex. To solve this issue, programming languages have a lot of predefined words that you can use anywhere in the code. These predefined words in Elixir can be special forms, *named functions*, or macros. We can also create our own named functions.

Named functions are defined inside of modules in Elixir. You can use an atom or *aliases* to name a module. An alias in Elixir is any word that starts with a capital letter, and only ASCII characters are allowed—for example, String, Integer, Enum, or IO. All aliases will transform into atoms during compile time with an Elixir prefix:

```
iex> String == :"Elixir.String"
true
```

Note that the atom :"Elixir.String" must have quotes because of the special character—in this example we're using a dot. You can invoke a function module by typing the name of the module and the name of the function using the dot operator between them. Try it:

```
iex> String.upcase("I'm using a module. Awesome!")
"I'M USING A MODULE. AWESOME!"
```

You can omit the parentheses by calling named functions. It's a matter of style over functionality. You should omit the parentheses when you want the code to be more readable, as in this example:

```
iex> IO.puts "Sometimes omitting the parentheses is better"
```

The way we call named functions is similar to the way we call anonymous functions, and we'll look at that next.

### Elixir's Named Functions

Elixir provides many useful modules, and all of them are documented online in the official Elixir documentation.[5] The table on page 25 lists shows some common ones that you can try in your IEx now to practice.

---

5.  https://hexdocs.pm/elixir/

| Module | Useful for | Examples |
| --- | --- | --- |
| String | Manipulating text | String.capitalize("hI Friends!"), String.downcase("OW") |
| Integer | Working with integers | Integer.parse("123"), Integer.to_string(-890), Integer.digits(890) |
| Float | Working with floats | Float.ceil(3.7), Float.floor(3.7), Float.round(3.7576, 2) |
| IO | Handling the input/output | IO.puts("Hello, World!"), IO.gets("What's your name?"), IO.inspect({:ok, 123}) |
| Kernel | Providing common functions | div(1, 2), rem(1, 2), is_number("Hi") |

The Kernel is a special Elixir module. Its functions are available to you without using the module name. If you look at the Kernel documentation,[6] you'll notice that all of operators and directives we have used and are going to use are defined there. You'll see also that all of them lead to functions. Elixir lets us use the Kernel functions without using the module name and providing operators with infix notations. However, fundamentally we're just calling functions.

## Creating Modules and Functions

We've seen some useful Elixir named functions. When we're writing applications, we may want to create our named functions to express our application's rules. The first step is to think about where we can create functions. We can imagine that a function is a box with things inside. We need to put that box somewhere. Then we have modules, which are big boxes that can accommodate functions. Modules are useful because we can put other modules inside of them. With this feature, we have the flexibility to organize our application to fit our needs.

We can create modules in our IEx sessions or in .ex files to be compiled. It's a good practice to keep our modules in files to facilitate their evolution. Let's create a file called checkout.ex. You can place the file anywhere you want. (In an Elixir project, we'd put the files in the lib directory, but you don't need to worry about it now; you'll see how to build a proper project in Chapter 6, *Designing Your Elixir Applications*, on page 105.) Then, after you create the file, we'll define our first module in it with a function that calculates the total cost of a product given its tax rate. Here's the file:

work_with_functions/lib/checkout.ex
```
defmodule Checkout do
end
```

---

6. https://hexdocs.pm/elixir/Kernel.html

Next we create a module called Checkout in the file. Note that the file name is the same as the module name, but the file name is lowercase. We use the .ex file extension for Elixir files that we want to compile. The defmodule indicates the beginning of the module definition. After this, we must add our module name. After it, we add do, which marks the beginning of the module body. Its definition ends with end.

Inside the module body, we can add code to invoke, import, or create functions. First let's focus on the definition of the functions by adding one to our module:

work_with_functions/lib/checkout.ex

```
defmodule Checkout do
  def total_cost(price, tax_rate) do
    price * (tax_rate + 1)
  end
end
```

We have added a function called total_cost. The def indicates the beginning of the function definition. After this, we must add our function name. The function name follows the same convention as variable names. We declare the function parameters inside of the parentheses. Then we add do, which marks the start of the function body. The function body definition ends with end. Inside the function body, we can add however many expressions we need. Like the anonymous functions, a named function returns the value of the last expression.

Notice that the naming convention is different between modules, functions, and variables. For modules, we use the *CamelCase* name format. This pattern says that every word in the compound name starts with a capital letter. For example, ShoppingCart, ProductBacklog, and CharacterSheet. The file names of the module, functions, and variables use *snake_case*. This pattern says that we should add an underscore (_) to separate the words in a compound name and the words must be lowercase. For example, the respective file names for the previous modules would be shopping_cart.ex, product_backlog.ex, and character_sheet.ex.

We can try our module using IEx. Open your session in the same directory of the module file:

```
iex> c("checkout.ex")
iex> Checkout.total_cost(100, 0.2)
120.0
```

The c function compiles the given file and provides the Checkout module to the current IEx session. Then we can call our module like any Elixir module we have tested before. We can define a function in a single line by using do optional syntax, like this:

```
defmodule Checkout do
  def total_cost(price, tax_rate), do: price * (tax_rate + 1)
end
```

In a large application, it can be confusing if the application modules' names are mixed with Elixir's modules. It's a good practice to start a new application by putting a name—a *namespace*—before each of the custom modules' names, separated by dots. That will prevent name collisions since each module must have a unique name. Try it:

work_with_functions/lib/ecommerce/checkout.ex
```
defmodule Ecommerce.Checkout do
  def total_cost(price, tax_rate) do
    price * (tax_rate + 1)
  end
end
```

You can also try it using IEx:

```
iex> c("checkout.ex")
iex> Ecommerce.Checkout.total_cost(100, 0.2)
120.0
```

Let's recap. In an Elixir project, we put a custom module in a file that has the same name as the module, but in lowercase, with one module per file. The modules go inside of a directory that has the same name of the module's namespace. For example, the Ecommerce.Checkout module has an ecommerce directory with a checkout.ex file inside. With this simple convention, our application can evolve with new modules, and they will be in the proper place. The names in a program are organized in namespaces.

## Importing Named Functions

The named functions we created work just like Elixir's provided functions. We can call any named function using the pattern ModuleName.name_of_the_function. Depending on the module we're creating, writing ModuleName all the time can be repetitive. We can reduce the code using the import directive. It works like the Kernel functions; we don't need to type the name of the module before every function name. Elixir imports all Kernel facilities to our programming environment by default.

Let's see how we can use the import directive to create a module that stores a list of tasks in a file. Since we'll have file manipulation, we'll use the File module.[7] Let's create a file called task_list.ex:

---

7.  https://hexdocs.pm/elixir/File.html

```
work_with_functions/lib/task_list.ex
defmodule TaskList do
  @file_name "task_list.md"

  def add(task_name) do
    task = "[ ] " <> task_name <> "\n"
    File.write(@file_name, task, [:append])
  end

  def show_list do
    File.read(@file_name)
  end
end
```

The TaskList module adds tasks and lists them. The add function creates a task by appending a line with its name to a file. The function show_list reads the file contents. Don't worry now about show_list's ugly output and the errors that may happen if you try to read a file that doesn't exist. In this code, we'll understand what the module attributes are and how to import the file functions.

Take a look at @file_name; it's a *module attribute*. Module attributes can be used as annotations, temporary storage, or constants. Here we're using the module attribute as a constant. It's a special type of variable that will be available in the entire module. It's helpful because if we want to change the file name, we only need to change it in one place.

We can reduce the necessity of writing File every time we call write or read functions by importing the module functions. Let's add the import directive to our TaskList module:

```
work_with_functions/lib/task_list_with_import.ex
defmodule TaskListWithImport do
  import File, only: [write: 3, read: 1]

  @file_name "task_list.md"

  def add(task_name) do
    task = "[ ] " <> task_name <> "\n"
    write(@file_name, task, [:append])
  end

  def show_list do
    read(@file_name)
  end
end
```

The number after the function name in the import directive is called the function *arity*. A function arity is the number of arguments a function receives. In the Elixir documentation, function arity is commonly expressed in this way:

name_of_the_function/arity—for example, File.read/1 or File.write/3. When we're importing a named function, we must always pass its name and its arity.

When we use import, we don't need to write the full name of the function. While that's a nice shortcut, we're being less explicit about where read and write functions came from. We can also use import without the only option, and it will implicitly import all functions. That can be a problem in a situation where we're importing multiple modules, because it will be hard to understand which module each function came from. In Elixir, developers prefer being explicit, writing the full name of the functions most of the time, using the only option when importing functions, and using the implicit import when you know the function names can't cause confusion.

## Using Named Functions as Values

When we're using anonymous functions, we have the option of binding them to variables or using them in arguments. What about named functions? Can we do the same? Let's try it:

```
iex> upcase = String.upcase
** (UndefinedFunctionError) undefined function String.upcase/0
```

Well, we can't do it this way. Elixir is trying to invoke a function String.upcase with an arity of zero; since parentheses are optional Elixir is trying to invoke a function without arguments. If we want to use String.upcase/1 like a value, we can wrap that function in an anonymous function. We'll create an anonymous function that will call String.upcase/1 delegating the given argument. Let's do it:

```
iex> upcase = fn string -> String.upcase(string) end
iex> upcase.("hello, world!")
"HELLO, WORLD!"
```

This is a common pattern in functional programming. Elixir provides a handy function-capturing operator. Using it, we can more easily use a named function as a value. Check it out:

```
iex> upcase = &String.upcase/1
iex> upcase.("hello, world!")
"HELLO, WORLD!"
```

Here we used the & operator to capture a reference to the function String.upcase/1, and the = operator to bind it to the upcase variable. The function that we pass to the operator must respect the pattern *function/arity*. It's a short way of binding named functions to variables or functions' arguments.

We can also use the & operator to create anonymous functions. Let's define the total_cost function using the capturing shortcut syntax:

```
iex> total_cost = &(&1 * &2)
iex> total_cost.(10, 2)
20
```

The & operator defines the beginning of the function, and its body is inside of the parentheses. There we have an expression that multiplies &1 by &2. &1 represents the first argument, and &2 the second. With this information, the Elixir compiler creates a function that receives two arguments, multiplying the first argument by the second. We can't use the capture syntax for creating anonymous functions with zero arity:

```
iex> check = &(true)
** (CompileError) tmp/src.exs:1: invalid args for &, expected an expression in
the format of &Mod.fun/arity, &local/arity or a capture containing at least one
argument as &1, got: true
```

In this case, we should use the explicit fn form:

```
iex> check = fn -> true end
iex> check.()
true
```

The parentheses are also optional:

```
iex> mult_by_2 = & &1 * 2
iex> mult_by_2.(3)
6
```

Use the capture syntax with caution, because its lack of argument names can affect your code readability. Using it too much will make your code hard to understand.

## Wrapping Up

In this chapter, we started with the basics of functional programming, from simple expressions to building named functions with modules. Let's review what we've done:

- We created simple expressions with Elixir values, literals, and operators.

- We created anonymous functions and used them as a new value type.

- We tested the variables' immutability and scope.

- We created named functions and learned how to import functions to our modules.

- We used named functions as values.

In the next chapter, we'll explore one of the most interesting features of functional programming: *pattern matching*. Learning how to use it will take your programming skills to a whole new level.

## Your Turn

- Create an expression that solves the following problem: Sarah has bought ten slices of bread for ten cents each, three bottles of milk for two dollars each, and a cake for fifteen dollars. How many dollars has Sarah spent?

- Bob has traveled 200 km in four hours. Using variables, print a message showing his travel distance, time, and average velocity.

- Build an anonymous function that applies a tax of 12% to a given price. It should print a message with the new price and tax value. Bind the anonymous function to a variable called apply_tax. You should use apply_tax with Enum.each/2, like in the following example. Don't worry about Enum.each/2 now; you'll see it in detail in Chapter 5, *Using Higher-Order Functions*, on page 81. You only need to know that Enum.each/2 will execute apply_tax in each item of a list.

```
Enum.each [12.5, 30.99, 250.49, 18.80], apply_tax
# Price: 14.0 - Tax: 1.5
# Price: 34.7088 - Tax: 3.7188
# Price: 280.5488 - Tax: 30.0588
# Price: 21.056 - Tax: 2.256
```

- Create a module called MatchstickFactory and a function called boxes/1. The function will calculate the number of boxes necessary to accommodate some matchsticks. It returns a map with the number of boxes necessary for each type of box. The factory has three types of boxes: the big ones hold fifty matchsticks, the medium ones hold twenty, and the small ones hold five. The boxes can't have fewer matchstick that they can hold; they must be full. The returning map should contain the remaining matchsticks. It should work like this:

```
MatchstickFactory.boxes(98)
# %{big: 1, medium: 2, remaining_matchsticks: 3, small: 1}
MatchstickFactory.boxes(39)
# %{big: 0, medium: 1, remaining_matchsticks: 4, small: 3}
```

Tip: You'll need to use the rem/2 and div/2 functions.[8] [9]

---

8. https://hexdocs.pm/elixir/Kernel.html#rem/2
9. https://hexdocs.pm/elixir/Kernel.html#div/2

# CHAPTER 3

# Using Pattern Matching to Control the Program Flow

Controlling the program flow means controlling which functions and expressions will be executed. Imperative languages rely mainly on conditional constructors like if, but here in the functional world, *pattern matching* plays the central role. However, pattern matching is often misunderstood and hard for beginners to comprehend. That's why half of this chapter is dedicated to understanding pattern matching. Then we'll use pattern matching to decide which function to dispatch so we can have a *control flow* mechanism. By the end of this chapter, we'll see some Elixir control-flow structures that use logical and pattern-matching expressions to simplify common expressions. Let's take the first step and learn about pattern matching.

## Making Two Things Match

Elixir's pattern matching shapes everything you program. It's useful for assigning variables, unpacking values, and making decisions such as which function to invoke. The basis of pattern matching is that it tries to make two things match, and it does something when it fails to do so.

You'll start to learn about pattern matching with the = operator. This operator raises a MatchError when it fails to match two things, stopping the program execution. Otherwise, when both sides of the operator have a match, the program keeps running. Let's see how it works in practice, step by step. Open an IEx session and type the following pattern-matching expression:

```
iex> 1 = 1
1
iex> 2 = 1
** (MatchError) no match of right hand side value: 1
iex> 1 = 2
** (MatchError) no match of right hand side value: 2
```

1 = 1 matches, but 2 = 1 and 1 = 2 don't because they're different numbers. Let's experiment with a familiar expression using variables:

```
iex> x = 1
1
```

You're probably saying to yourself, "What a disappointment! It's just a variable assignment!" Maybe you're thinking it's a joke. But it's not. It's pattern matching. Elixir is making both sides equivalent by binding the value 1 to the variable x. Let's try something different:

```
iex> 1 = x
1
```

The value is on the left side, the variable is on the right side, and it's a valid Elixir expression. It's fascinating, right? We said previously that x = 1, and now the value 1 is bound to the x variable. When we type 1 = x, Elixir tries to check if the value on the left side is equal to the right side. If the two sides are equal, then we have a valid expression. Let's look at another example:

```
iex> 2 = x
** (MatchError) no match of the right hand side value: 1
```

Elixir tries to match both sides. The value of the variable on the right side is the number 1. The number 2 isn't equal to 1, and it results in a MatchError. The process of checking if both sides of the = operator are equivalent is pattern matching. It can be hard to understand if this is the first time you've seen it. To help you understand what's happening in the background, let's look at an improvised imperative version of the preceding expression:

```
if 2 == x
  2
else
  raise MatchError
end
```

If x is not equal to 2, it raises an error. Now let's see what happens when we try to invert the sides of that expression:

```
iex> x = 2
2
```

Now that the variable x is on the left side, the behavior is different. When the variable is on the left side, Elixir will match everything, binding the value of the expression on the right side to the variable. We can bind new values for existing variables. We call that *rebinding*. Elixir binds the number 2 to x to make both sides match. We can avoid the rebinding by using the pin operator: ^. That operator lets you avoid the rebinding by using the value of the variable to run the matching. Try the operator by yourself:

```
iex> x = 2
2
iex> ^x = 2
2
iex> ^x = 1
** (MatchError) no match of right hand side value: 1
```

With the pin operator, Elixir uses the value of the variable to match. Using this simple = operator for pattern matching, we can check if both sides of that operator have a match. When they don't match, the program stops the execution with a matching error. Realizing that = isn't just for binding variables can be hard if you're accustomed to variable assignments in other programming paradigms. To help you in this transition, you can use an algebra analogy: if x = 1, then 1 = x is valid. The pattern matching doesn't stop here. We can create checks and unpack values of different types of data, allowing us to solve more complex problems.

## Unpacking Values from Various Data Types

Pattern matching is also useful for extracting parts of values to variables in a process called *destructuring*. It's our primary tool to get a string part, an item from a list, and a value from the map. We use destructuring together with pattern matching when we're making two things match. In this section, we'll explore pattern matching with several data types and see how we can extract values and make more complex matches.

### Matching Parts of a String

Strings are a data type that we can use in pattern matching. We can use the <> operator to check the beginning of a string. It's useful for checking text that's organized in key/value pairs. For example, we can match one header pattern in the HTTP protocol. In the following example, we'll make a simple match to get the credentials part of the following string:

```
iex> "Authentication: " <> credentials = "Authentication: Basic dXNlcjpwYXNz"
iex> credentials
"Basic dXNlcjpwYXNz"
```

The only restriction in pattern matching with strings is that we can't use a variable on the left side of the <> operator. Consider this example:

```
iex> first_name <> " Doe" = "John Doe"
** (CompileError) a binary field without size is only allowed at the end of a
binary pattern and never allowed in binary generators
```

Strings are binaries, and <> is a binary operator. The error means we can't start our expression with a variable without providing its binary size. It's saying that we can't check the end of a string. We can easily avoid this by reversing the string values. Take a look:

```
iex> "eoD " <> first_name  = String.reverse("John Doe")
iex> String.reverse(first_name)
"John"
```

Using the workaround String.reverse, we have matched the string when the last name is *Doe* and extracted the first name to a variable. It's an unusual solution—you can create better matchings for strings by using Elixir regular expressions. If you want to know more, take a look at the Regex module.[1]

Strings are binaries in Elixir. You can also use binary pattern-matching syntax to achieve powerful and fast checks. We won't cover binary pattern matching in this book, but you can consult the Elixir official Getting Started guide to understand how it works.[2]

## Matching Tuples

Tuples are collections that are stored contiguously in memory, allowing fast access to their elements by index. They are common in functions, results, and messages sent to processes in Elixir's core and community libraries. They are often used to pass a signal with values. For example, we can use a tuple to say whether the result of a function was a success or a failure, where the first item indicates the success with an atom and the second item is a computed value:

```
{:ok, 42}
{:error, :not_found}
```

Here is an illustration of how tuples are stored in memory:

| index: 0 | index: 1 | index: 0 | index: 1 |
|----------|----------|----------|------------|
| :ok | 42 | :error | :not_found |

---

1.   https://hexdocs.pm/elixir/Regex.html
2.   http://elixir-lang.org/getting-started/binaries-strings-and-char-lists.html#binaries-and-bitstrings

We can store items in a tuple and bind them to variables with a simple expression. Try it:

```
iex> {a, b, c} = {4, 5, 6}
{4, 5, 6}
iex> a
4
iex> b
5
iex> c
6
```

To make the left side match the right side of the expression, Elixir has done multiple variable bindings. Now the variables a, b, and c have the values of the elements in the tuple. It's destructuring in action again. We're unpacking values from the tuple and binding them to variables.

Tuples are also useful for signaling successes and failures in a function's return. We can create a function that returns a tuple, where the first item will be an :ok, indicating success. Then we can use pattern matching only to let the program run when the result is successful. Try the following code to see this in action:

```
iex> process_life_the_universe_and_everything = fn -> {:ok, 42} end
iex> {:ok, answer} = process_life_the_universe_and_everything.()
iex> IO.puts "The answer is #{answer}."
The answer is 42.
```

The function process_life_the_universe_and_everything returns a tuple. The first element indicates success with an :ok atom, and the second item is the computed value. We have matched it using the {:ok, answer} pattern. The pattern is a tuple that expects the first item will be :ok and the second item will bind to the variable answer. Then we printed the value of answer. This is how we can use tuples and pattern matching to check more complex structures than numbers or strings.

---

**Functions Might Not Be Consistent When Returning Tuples**

Elixir's functions might be inconsistent when returning values to indicate error or success. For example, some functions can return an atom for the unsuccessful result and a tuple for a successful one. It depends on what the creator of that function was trying to express. It's always good to check the documentation before using a function. A good practice—one that's very common in Elixir's functions and community libraries—is to return {:ok, value} for success and {:error, :error_type} for failure.

We'll create an example using Integer.parse/1 and see how we can use tuples in different ways. Let's build a script that helps paper-and-pen role-playing game (RPG) players calculate the abilities of their characters. In an RPG, players create and play roles in stories that they build together. Some players use books with complicated rules about how they can make their characters, and our script will help them.

A player types the number of her character's ability score, and the program shows the modifier value. Abilities and modifiers? If you've never played an RPG, don't worry. The most important part of this exercise is building a program in which users can input a number that will be computed only when the number is valid. It's hard to predict all the things users will type. For example, someone could type *hot dogs* and our program would stop with an error. We want to ensure the program only does the math with valid numbers. Let's create an Elixir script file called ability_modifier.exs. Write the following program:

pattern_matching/lib/ability_modifier.exs
```
user_input = IO.gets "Write your ability score:\n"
{ability_score, _} = Integer.parse(user_input)
ability_modifier = (ability_score - 10) / 2
IO.puts "Your ability modifier is #{ability_modifier}"
```

The .exs extension is for Elixir scripts that don't need to generate a compiled version. It's useful for simple scripts. The wildcard character _ in the {ability_score, _} expression matches everything. It's used to ignore some parts of the matching expression. We use the IO.gets/1 function to get user input—they need to press Enter to send their input. We can run this script using the elixir ability_modifier.exs command and interact with it:

```
‹ Write your ability score:
⇒ 16
‹ Your ability modifier is 3.0
```

You can execute the script again and generate an error by typing *hot dogs*, just for fun.

Now let's discuss the tuple pattern on the second line of the script. The Integer.parse/1 functions return a tuple for a successful parsing. The first element is the parsed value and the second item is the remaining text that wasn't parsed. When the input can't be parsed to an integer, the function doesn't return a tuple; it returns an atom :error.

Notice that here we don't have an atom saying the result was successful; a tuple is enough to describe it. Then we use the pattern-matching expression {ability_score, _} to check if the result is a tuple—in other words, if the parsing

### The Difference Between the Various Equals Operators

In Elixir we have many equals operators that have different use cases. = is used for pattern matching. == returns true when the elements are equal and when integers and floats are equivalent numbers. === returns true when arguments are equivalent and have the same type. Here are some examples:

```
1 = 1 # returns 1
2 = 1 # match error!
1 == 1.0 # returns true
2 == 1 # returns false
1.0 === 1.0 # returns true
1.0 === 1 # returns false
```

was successful. This expression also binds the first element to the variable ability_score and ignores the remaining text using the wildcard. That's how we can use pattern matching with tuples to extract values and make some matches.

## Matching Lists

Tuples are for representing collections of a few items. We've used pattern matching on them, taken values, and put them in variables. But tuples have one limitation: they're stored contiguously in memory. We need to know in advance how many elements are inside of them. It's a problem because we can't always predict a collection size and it's impractical to write all the items of a vast collection in an expression. To address these problems, Elixir uses the *list* data type. In Elixir, lists are *linked lists*. That means each item of the collection contains a value and an implicit reference to the next element. For a list [:a, :b, :c, :d, :e], we'll have something like this in memory:

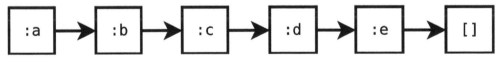

A list ends by linking to an empty list, turning the list into a *proper list*. It's useful to avoid infinite loops by checking if the last item is a empty list and stopping a recursive iteration. In some rare cases you can face an *improper list*—one that doesn't link to an empty list at its end.

Like with tuples, we can create pattern-matching expressions to extract values from the collection and put them into variables or check if the list items are following some pattern. For representing lists, we use the [] syntax. Let's start our exploration by creating an expression that tells if the items are the same. Let's try it in our IEx:

```
iex> [a, a, a] = [1, 1, 1]
[1, 1, 1]
iex> [a, a, a] = [1, 2, 1]
** (MatchError) no match of right hand side value: [1, 2, 1]
iex> [a, b, a] = [1, 2, 1]
[1, 2, 1]
iex> [a, a, a] = ["apples", "apples", "apples"]
["apples", "apples", "apples"]
```

The pattern [a, a, a] means that a list must have three elements with the same value. We see this because we're using the variable a for the three items. Variables have a unique value in an expression; the variable a can't be the number 1 and 2 at the same time. That's why the list [1, 2, 1] results in a MatchError with [a, a, a] but succeeds with [a, b, a]. We can create complex checks like this one:

```
iex> [a, a, "pineapples"] = ["apples", "apples", "pineapples"]
["apples", "apples", "pineapples"]
```

The pattern [a, a, "pineapples"] means the first two list items must be the same value, and the third item must be *pineapples*. It demonstrates how we can use values in list patterns.

When we want to ignore some parts of a list, we can use the wildcard character _. Type this in your IEx to see it in action:

```
iex> [_, a, _] = [10, 2, 12]
iex> a
2
iex> [_, a, a] = [16, 4, 4]
iex> a
4
```

We've used the wildcard character to tell Elixir that we don't want it to check certain elements. The wildcard character isn't exclusive to lists. It can be utilized in all pattern-matching expressions and data types.

Elixir provides a special | operator for lists. When we use it, we can separate some elements of the list from the rest, enabling us to work with collections of unknown size. Knowing that, open your IEx. Let's try separating some list elements using the | operator:

```
iex> [ head | tail ] = [:a, :b, :c, :d]
iex> head
:a
iex> tail
[:b, :c, :d]
```

The left side of the | operator matches the first items of a list; in this case, we're matching only one. The right side always matches the rest of the elements. We bound the first item to the variable head and the rest to the variable tail. (When working with lists, the names *head* for the first element and *tail* for the rest are common.) We have extracted values from the list without worrying about its size, separating the first element from the rest of the list.

Let's check what happens when we use the | operator in lists that have one element. Can you guess the values of head and tail? Try it in your IEx:

```
iex> [ head | tail ] = [:a]
```

head has the value :a, and tail has an empty list. After Elixir extracts the unique element to the variable head, all that's left is an empty list. See what happens if you use this operator in an empty list in your IEx:

```
iex> [ head | tail ] = []
** (MatchError) no match of right hand side value: []
```

Since we can't separate an element of an empty list, it turns into an impossible operation. When that happens, MatchError is raised. We can extract more than one element on the left side of the | operator . Try it in your IEx:

```
iex> [ a, b | rest ] = [1, 2, 3, 4]
iex> a
1
iex> b
2
iex> rest
[3, 4]
```

We're binding the first two elements to the variables a and b. We could bind more variables or use the same names of the variables to check some patterns. Using the | operator to access subparts of lists frees us from worry about list size. We can explore it more, like how to apply a computation on each list item, but let's save it for the next chapters.

## Matching Maps

Maps are data types structured in key/value pairs. They are used to represent a set of values with labels that need to stay together. For example, if we want to represent a user signup, we can use a map to store the fields and their values in memory, like this:

```
iex> user_signup = %{email: "johndoe@mail.com", password: "12345678"}
```

The %{} is the syntax to create map values. email: is the key and expands to an atom. "johndoe@mail.com" is the value of the key :email. The equivalent alternative syntax uses =>:

```
iex> user_signup = %{:email => "johndoe@mail.com", :password => "12345678"}
```

It's little bit verbose, but this syntax is useful for storing any value in a key. For example,

```
iex> sales = %{"2017/01" => 2000, "2017/02" => 2500}
```

We can also represent complex nested structures:

```
%{
  name: "John Doe",
  age: 20,
  programming_languages: ["Ruby", "Elixir", "JavaScript", "Java"],
  location: %{city: "São Paulo", country: "Brazil", state: "SP"}
}
```

We can check values and keys of maps by using pattern matching. Try the following example in your IEx:

```
iex> abilities = %{strength: 16, dexterity: 12, intelligence: 10}
iex> %{strength: strength_value} = abilities
iex> strength_value
16
```

In this example, we're accessing the key :strength and binding its value to the variable strength_value. The pattern-matching expression always checks a subset of the map, which means we don't need to provide all the keys for a match to be successful. We can use only the keys that we need. If the map doesn't have the key, a MatchError will arise. Check it out:

```
iex> %{wisdom: wisdom_value} = abilities
** (MatchError) no match of right hand side value...
```

If we use an empty map, it will match all maps. For example,

```
iex> %{} = abilities
%{dexterity: 12, intelligence: 10, strength: 16}
iex> %{} = %{a: 1, b: 2}
%{a: 1, b: 2}
```

We can use pattern-matching expressions to extract and check values at the same time. Let's demonstrate this by creating an expression using the same variable, abilities, from the previous example. Try this new pattern in your IEx:

```
iex> %{intelligence: 10, dexterity: dexterity_value} = abilities
iex> dexterity_value
12
```

We're telling Elixir that the abilities variable must have an :intelligence key with the number 10. At the same time, we're telling Elixir to check if the :dexterity key exists and, if so, to extract its value to a variable.

We can use the = operator on the left side of the pattern-matching expression to check and bind at the same time. Try it:

```
iex> %{strength: strength_value = 16 } = abilities
iex> strength_value
16
```

To understand it, look at strength_value = 16 in isolation. The expression binds the 16 value to the strength_value variable. Knowing that strength_value is 16, it will try to match against the abilities structure. The abilities structure has the key and value strength: 16. It matches! We could do the same thing in two steps:

```
iex> strength_value = 16
iex> %{strength: ^strength_value} = abilities
```

Here we used the pin operator to match abilities using the value of the strength_value variable. Use the one-step version for simple assignments, and use the two-step version when you have some calculation or function call on the variables assignment. This way, your code will be easy to understand.

## Maps vs. Keyword Lists

A keyword list is a list of two-element tuples: it allows duplicated keys but they must be atoms. We match them using the list syntax:

```
iex> [b, c] = [a: 1, a: 12]
iex> b
{:a, 1}
iex> c
{:a, 12}
```

Maps are structures that allow any value to be the key, but the key must be unique. Keywords are useful for function options; for example, the import directive takes a keyword list because named functions in Elixir can have identical names but with different arity. For example,

```
iex> import String, only: [pad_leading: 2, pad_leading: 3]
String
iex> pad_leading("def", 6)
"   def"
iex> pad_leading("def", 6, "-")
"---def"
```

Keyword lists permit you to create structures with identical keys but with different values. Meanwhile, maps are useful for things like representing database rows, because column names are unique in a table. Here are some examples:

```
x = %{a: 1, a: 12} # result in {a: 12}
x = [a: 1, a: 12] # OK
x = [{:a, 1}, {:a, 12}] # it's the same above
x = %{1 => :a, 2 => :b } # OK
x = [1 => :a, 2 => :b] # syntax error
```

The syntax of maps and keywords is very similar, but their limitations make them handy for different use cases.

## Matching Structs

Structs are extensions of mapping structures. They are useful for representing consistent structures that have the same set of keys everywhere in the application. All structs have a list of permitted attributes. It's impossible to create a struct with a key that's not in the list of allowed attributes because Elixir provides a *compile-time* guarantee. For example, take a look at the official documentation of the Date struct.[3] It has the following fields: year, month, day, and calendar. We can't create a Date struct with a key hot_dog. Using a struct for dates guarantees all dates in Elixir to have a consistent structure.

Let's use pattern matching to extract the values of a struct. We can use the same %{} syntax that we have used with maps. After all, structs are extensions of maps. Try the following code in your IEx:

```
iex> date = ~D[2018-01-01]
iex> %{year: year} = date
iex> year
2018
```

Pattern matching with structs works like it does with maps. This means we can use everything we've learned about maps on structs. The date *sigil* ~D is new here. Sigils are shortcuts to create values with a simplified text representation. For example, with the word-list sigil we could create a list of candies without worrying about double quotes and commas:

```
iex> ~w(chocolate jelly mint)
["chocolate", "jelly", "mint"]
```

That sigil considers each word a string, and a whitespace separates each item of the list. We won't explore all sigils available in Elixir and how to customize them, but you can learn more about them in the Elixir official guide.[4]

---

3.   https://hexdocs.pm/elixir/Date.html
4.   http://elixir-lang.org/getting-started/sigils.html

There is only one fundamental difference between structs and maps: The name of the struct can be used to indicate which type of structure we're expecting. Try this in your IEx:

```
iex> date = ~D[2018-01-01]
iex> %Date{day: day} = date
iex> day
1
iex> %Date{day: day} = %{day: 1}
** (MatchError) no match of right hand side value: %{day: 1}
```

In the first attempt, the match works because we're matching a Date struct. The second attempt doesn't work even though the map structure is valid, because the value is a map and not a Date. With this check, we can ensure that we're working with the expected type, and our program can run safely.

## Control Flow with Functions

Programs typically cover a variety of scenarios, and we need to create code to handle each one. In functional programming, pattern matching and functions are the fundamental tools we use to control the program flow. Until now, we've used pattern matching with the = operator to make two things match. It's useful for making sure our program runs in an expected scenario. When the match is not possible, Elixir raises an error and stops the program process. When we use pattern matching with functions, we can do more than just throw errors, and that's what we'll discuss in this section.

Let's create a simple program that, given two numbers, will say which one is greater. If the numbers are equal, we can show either one of them. For this example we'll use named functions, then create a file number_compare.ex and type the following:

pattern_matching/lib/number_compare.ex
```
defmodule NumberCompare do
  def greater(number, other_number) do
    check(number >= other_number, number, other_number)
  end

  defp check(true, number, _), do: number
  defp check(false, _, other_number), do: other_number
end
```

We have new stuff here: multiple function definitions with the same name—some of them defined with a defp directive, and others with values in the arguments. Don't worry about those details right now. The main thing here is that we've created multiple functions with different values in their arguments. Before we discuss the code in detail, let's see it in action. Run this in your IEx:

```
iex> c("number_compare.ex")
iex> NumberCompare.greater(6, 2)
6
iex> NumberCompare.greater(1, 8)
8
iex> NumberCompare.greater(2, 2)
2
```

Let's examine the greater function first: we used the >= operator to compare two numbers. It will be true when the first number is greater than or equal to the second number, and false when the second number is the greater. We needed to create code that handles these two possibilities. Then we created an auxiliary function check to help us achieve the solution.

We created two versions of check, each one to handle a possibility of the Boolean result: one for the true case and the other for the false case. It's possible because, in Elixir functions, the arguments can be pattern-matching expressions.

Let's see the first definition of check again:

pattern_matching/lib/number_compare.ex
```
defp check(true, number, _), do: number
```

The first parameter is matching the true value. This function will handle the case when the first number is the greater. Then we bind the higher number to the variable number. The third argument is for the lower number; we don't need it and we tell Elixir that by using a wildcard for this argument. In the function body, we return the number variable. Now we've covered the first possibility.

Let's look at the second one:

pattern_matching/lib/number_compare.ex
```
defp check(false, _, other_number), do: other_number
```

We're using pattern matching to check if the first argument is false, meaning the second number is the greater. We use the wildcard for the lower number to tell Elixir that number doesn't matter. Then we bind the higher number to the variable other_number. In the function body, we return the other_number variable. By creating it, we have covered the second possibility, of the second number being the greater.

That's it! We've handled both possibilities using functions and pattern matching. In Elixir we call these multiple function definitions *function clauses*.

We can create as many function clauses as we need. The only requirement is that they must be defined in sequence. This means we can't create another function between the check clauses' definitions. When we call a function name with multiple definitions, the order of the function clauses is very important—Elixir will execute the function of the first clause that matches.

Let's look at our entry function greater/2 again:

pattern_matching/lib/number_compare.ex
```
def greater(number, other_number) do
  check(number >= other_number, number, other_number)
end
```

We call the helper function check/3, passing the result of the >= operator in the first argument, and the numbers in the second and third arguments. With this strategy, the helper function clauses can handle the Boolean value and return the greater number. Other developers who may want to use this functionality in other modules only need to use the greater/2 version. The check/3 is an internal function that helps us achieve our goal, so the other modules don't need to know about it. We can enforce that using the defp directive.

defp defines private functions of your module. Private functions are useful for controlling the accessibility of the functions from outside. They can't even be imported from other modules. If in our IEx session we try to call the check/3 function, an UndefinedFunctionError is raised. Let's try it:

```
iex> NumberCompare.check(true, 2, 2)
** (UndefinedFunctionError)
```

At this point, we've covered a lot of pattern-matching expressions, and we can use all of them in function arguments. I don't need to explain every pattern because they work the same, but it's a good idea to keep practicing.

## Applying Default Values for Functions

We can apply a default value to named function arguments using the \\ operator. When we apply a default value to an argument in a function, Elixir creates two versions of that function. In the first version, the argument marked with the default value will not have a value, so it's mandatory that it be supplied. In the second version the argument doesn't exist; internally Elixir will invoke the first function version, passing the default value. Take a look at how it works in practice:

```
defmodule Checkout do
  def total_cost(price, quantity \\ 10), do: price * quantity
end
```

Try it in your IEx session:

```
iex> c("checkout.ex")
iex> Checkout.total_cost(12)
120
iex> Checkout.total_cost(12, 5)
60
```

When we don't provide the second argument, Elixir uses the default value. We can only have one default value for each parameter. If we try to define multiple function clauses with different default values, Elixir will generate a compile error. In the background, Elixir is creating multiple functions with different arities. We have two different functions: Checkout.total_cost/1 and Checkout.total_cost/2. We can see these different functions when we try it to capture them:

```
iex> using_default = &Checkout.total_cost/1
iex> not_using_default = &Checkout.total_cost/2
iex> using_default.(12)
120
iex> using_default.(12, 4)
** (BadArityError)
iex> not_using_default.(12)
** (BadArityError)
iex> not_using_default.(12, 5)
60
```

Let's make clear what happens in the background by generating equivalent code without using the \\ shortcut. It will be like this:

```
defmodule Checkout do
  def total_cost(price), do: total_cost(price, 10)
  def total_cost(price, quantity), do: price * quantity
end
```

total_cost/1 passes the default quantity 10 to total_cost/2. In Elixir, functions have fixed arity. Functions with the same name but with a different number of parameters are different functions. We consider the arity to be part of the function's unique name, which is why we reference arities with name_of_the_function/arity notation.

## Expanding Control with Guard Clauses

Creating multiple functions with pattern matching to control the program flow can be exhausting sometimes. In the example where we created the NumberCompare module, we have to build auxiliary functions to handle the >= operation result. Creating too many functions for trivial tasks can generate code that is hard to maintain. We can improve this using Elixir guard clauses.

Guard clauses permit us to add Boolean expressions in our functions, adding more power to our function clauses.

We can create guard clauses by using the when keyword after functions' parameters. Let's see how it works for improving our NumberCompare code:

pattern_matching/lib/guard_clauses/number_compare.ex
```
defmodule NumberCompare do
  def greater(number, other_number) when number >= other_number, do: number
  def greater(_, other_number), do: other_number
end
```

We can try the code above using IEx:

```
iex> c("number_compare.ex")
iex> NumberCompare.greater(2, 8)
8
```

We've used the guard clauses to check which number is greater; one function returns the first number, and the other returns the second. The expression when number >= other_number is the guard clause. When it's true, the function will be executed, returning the variable number. When the expression is false, it will try to run the second function clause. The second clause will always match because it doesn't have any check to prevent execution.

Guard clauses help us to create better function signatures, reducing the need for function helpers. We can also use guard clauses to enforce which data we're expecting. Let's improve the Checkout module that we created in the previous chapter. It calculates the total cost of a product, applying a tax rate. It's good to establish that neither of these numbers can be negative. Type the following module in your checkout.ex file:

pattern_matching/lib/guard_clauses/checkout.ex
```
defmodule Checkout do
  def total_cost(price, tax_rate) when price >= 0 and tax_rate >= 0 do
    price * (tax_rate + 1)
  end
end
```

The price >= 0 and tax_rate >= 0 expression ensures they must be positives. We can try the module using IEx:

```
iex> c("checkout.ex")
iex> Checkout.total_cost(40, 0.1)
44.0
iex> Checkout.total_cost(-2, 0.2)
** (FunctionClauseError) no function clause matching
iex> Checkout.total_cost(42.3, "Hello, World!")
** (ArithmeticError) bad argument in arithmetic expression
```

We tried our guard clauses with different inputs, passing positive numbers, and everything works great. When we tried to use negative numbers, it failed with the FunctionClauseError, which means we have no total_cost/2 that handles negative numbers. When we tried to pass the "Hello, World!", the error was different. The ArithmeticError happened in the price * (tax_rate + 1) expression, which means the text "Hello, World" passed the guard check; in other words, "Hello, World! is greater than 0.

Comparing a string to a number may look strange, but Elixir can compare text, numbers, and other types. This makes it practical to sort lists with mixed item types, and it's why the guard check passed. In Elixir, we don't need to be very defensive about types. It's a dynamically typed language and it is uncommon for developers to create functions with long guard-clause expressions just for type checking. If you want to have type safety in some functions, Elixir provides useful functions—for example, Kernel.is_integer/1 to check if a value is an integer.

---

**Elixir and Type Declaration**

Elixir is a dynamically typed language; the compiler never uses type specifications to optimize or modify the code. This means that when we program with Elixir, we don't need to worry about type declaration for every function or variable definition. Instead, we use automated tests and pattern matching to ensure we have a working piece of software. But at the same time, type specifications can be useful for creating documentation, and they have static analysis to find inconsistencies and possible bugs. If you want to learn more about type-specification tools in Elixir, consult the official documentation.[5]

---

You can use pattern matching and guard clauses in anonymous function arguments, as well. We use the -> operator between the function clause and the body. The following example rewrites the function NumberCompare.check/2 in the anonymous version:

```
number_compare = fn
  number, other_number when number >= other_number -> number
  _, other_number -> other_number
end

number_compare.(1, 2) # returns 2
```

You can see a list of functions and operators allowed in guard clauses in the Elixir official documentation.[6] You can't use standard functions in guard

---

5.    https://hexdocs.pm/elixir/typespecs.html
6.    https://elixir-lang.org/getting-started/case-cond-and-if.html#expressions-in-guard-clauses

clauses because the algorithm that checks which arguments match needs to be very fast and have no side effects to be practical. It means that only functions that are pure and fast are allowed. Erlang and Elixir ensure purity and speed by creating a list of authorized functions. That list can be expanded with Elixir macro functions.

Let's use macro functions to create a program that says if a number is even or odd. Elixir has functions that will help do the job. They are localized in a special section called *Macros* in the Elixir integer documentation.[7] The functions is_even/1 and is_odd/1 are what we're looking for. Create a file called even_or_odd.ex and type the following code:

`pattern_matching/lib/guard_clauses/even_or_odd.ex`
```
defmodule EvenOrOdd do
  require Integer

  def check(number) when Integer.is_even(number), do: "even"
  def check(number) when Integer.is_odd(number), do: "odd"
end
```

We can run it using IEx:

```
iex> c("even_or_odd.ex")
iex> EvenOrOdd.check(42)
"even"
iex> EvenOrOdd.check(43)
"odd"
```

The new thing here is the directive require. We need to use it because is_even/1 and is_odd/1 are macro functions. When you use a macro, it generates code before evaluating it. For example, when we use Integer.is_even(2), it generates the code (2 &&& 1) == 0 during the compilation phase. Then when we run the code the expression will be evaluated to true. Elixir's compiler needs the require directive to use the module in the compilation phase. The other important aspect of the require directive is that it's lexically scoped. Take a look:

`pattern_matching/lib/lexical/even_or_odd.ex`
```
defmodule EvenOrOdd do
  def is_even(number) do
    require Integer
    Integer.is_even(number)
  end

  def is_odd(number), do: Integer.is_odd(number)
end
```

---

7.　https://hexdocs.pm/elixir/Integer.html#macros

require Integer is in the EvenOrOdd.is_even/1 function, and the lexical scope means that Integer macro functions are available only there. The EvenOrOdd.is_odd/1 function is trying to use the Integer macro functions. If we attempt to compile it, we'll get a compile error complaining about the missing require Integer in the EvenOrOdd.is_odd/1 function.

&&& is the bitwise operator AND. It checks each value bit by bit, and sets the value to 1 when both bits are 1. Thanks to it, when you use the bitwise AND with 1, if a number is odd the final result is 1. The bitwise operators are beyond the scope of this book, but you can learn more about them in Elixir's official documentation.[8]

You can easily create macro functions to be used in guard clauses with the defguard directive. It's very handy to reuse common guard clauses in your modules. For example, let's add a new function to the Checkout module and reuse the guard checks:

pattern_matching/lib/guard_clauses/macro/checkout.ex

```
defmodule Checkout do
  defguard is_rate(value) when is_float(value) and value >= 0 and value <= 1
  defguard is_cents(value) when is_integer(value) and value >= 0

  def total_cost(price, tax_rate) when is_cents(price) and is_rate(tax_rate) do
    price + tax_cost(price, tax_rate)
  end

  def tax_cost(price, tax_rate) when is_cents(price) and is_rate(tax_rate) do
    price * tax_rate
  end
end
```

You can try the code above:

```
iex> c("checkout.ex")
iex> Checkout.tax_cost(40, 0.1)
4.0
iex> Checkout.total_cost(40, 0.1)
44.0
iex> Checkout.tax_cost(-2, 0.2)
** (FunctionClauseError) no function clause matching
iex> Checkout.total_cost(42.3, "Hello, World!")
** (FunctionClauseError) no function clause matching
```

Macro functions enable Elixir programmers to create more functions to be used in guard clauses. The only rule is that the generated code must respect the list of allowed functions in guard clauses. Macros are part of Elixir

---

8.    https://hexdocs.pm/elixir/Bitwise.html

metaprogramming, a great subject that's beyond the scope of this book; you can read more about it in the official Elixir getting-started guide.[9]

# Elixir Control-Flow Structures

Working with functional programming, we use function clauses to control the flow of the program. It's the expected behavior of a functional programmer, but it doesn't mean we can't use some Elixir built-in control-flow structures, such as case, cond, if, and unless, to develop features quickly. We'll see how each one can be useful and how it works.

## Case: Control with Pattern Matching

case is useful when we want to check an expression with multiple pattern-matching clauses. It's helpful for dealing with functions that may have an unexpected effect. To see how it works, we'll change our script that calculates the abilities modifier for RPG players:

```
pattern_matching/lib/elixir_flows/case/ability_modifier.exs
user_input = IO.gets "Write your ability score:\n"
case Integer.parse(user_input) do
  :error -> IO.puts "Invalid ability score: #{user_input}"
  {ability_score, _} ->
    ability_modifier = (ability_score - 10) / 2
    IO.puts "Your ability modifier is #{ability_modifier}"
end
```

We can run it with the elixir ability_modifier.exs command and interact with it:

```
❮ Write your ability score:
⇒ hot dogs
❮ Invalid ability score: hot dogs
```

We used case to handle two scenarios: one in which the user input is a valid number, and the other in which the user provides invalid information. We start to make the decision with the case directive. Then we add our expression that we want to match the result. All lines after do can be used to create clauses. We put the pattern-matching expression before the -> operator, and the expression to be evaluated after it. It can be one line (adding the code right after the ->) or multiple lines (if we create a line break). When a pattern-matching expression passes, the expression associated with it will be executed, and no more pattern-matching expressions will be evaluated.

---

9. https://elixir-lang.org/getting-started/meta/macros.html

The case directive returns the result of the expression that was evaluated. Knowing that, we can refactor our script to take advantage of it and write the code IO.puts once. Take a look:

pattern_matching/lib/elixir_flows/case_value/ability_modifier.exs
```
user_input = IO.gets "Write your ability score: "

result = case Integer.parse(user_input) do
  :error ->
    "Invalid ability score: #{user_input}"
  {ability_score, _} ->
    ability_modifier = (ability_score - 10) / 2
    "Your ability modifier is #{ability_modifier}"
end

IO.puts result
```

It's a good practice to use the case returning value; in the preceding example, we'd need to modify the code in only one place to change where the result will be printed. Like in functions, we can use guard clauses in the case control flow. Let's change our script again to indicate that the ability score must be a positive number:

pattern_matching/lib/elixir_flows/case_guard/ability_modifier.exs
```
result = case Integer.parse(user_input) do
  :error ->
    "Invalid ability score: #{user_input}"
  {ability_score, _} when ability_score >= 0 ->
    ability_modifier = (ability_score - 10) / 2
    "Your ability modifier is #{ability_modifier}"
end
```

Now that part of the code will be executed only if ability_score is greater than 0. Remember, when using the case control flow, if neither of the lines matches, an error will be raised and your process will stop.

## Cond: Control with Logical Expressions

The cond control flow is useful when you want to check different variables and values in logical expressions. That's useful when you don't need pattern matching for solving a problem.

Let's create a script that checks a person's age and says if that person is a kid, a teen, or an adult. Create check_age.exs:

pattern_matching/lib/elixir_flows/check_age.exs
```
{age, _} = Integer.parse IO.gets("Person's age:\n")

result = cond do
 age < 13 -> "kid"
 age <= 18 -> "teen"
```

```
  age > 18 -> "adult"
end

IO.puts "Result: #{result}"
```

We can interact with this script by running elixir check_age.exs:

```
❮ Person's age:
⇒ 12
❮ Result: kid
```

We've used the cond structure to verify each age range and evaluate the description. Each line of our cond structure is composed of a condition and its associated expression. It's similar to how the case structure works. When a condition evaluates to something truthy, the code associated with it will be executed. Remember, something truthy in Elixir is everything that is not nil or false.

The last condition is important. If it doesn't return something truthy it will raise an error. When you don't want to create an overhead of functions for simple tasks, the cond control flow can help you out.

## Taking a Look at Our Old Friend if

All the popular languages have an if control flow, and Elixir is no different. if is very useful when you want to execute a command when some expression results in a truthy value. Let's do a quick overview of the building blocks using the number-comparison example. Let's rewrite our NumberCompare.greater/2 function:

```
pattern_matching/lib/elixir_flows/if/number_compare.ex
defmodule NumberCompareWithIf do
  def greater(number, other_number) do
    if number >= other_number do
      number
    else
      other_number
    end
  end
end
```

When the expression in if is truthy, the subsequent block will execute; otherwise, it will be the else block.

unless is common in Ruby and works the same way in Elixir. It's similar to the if construction, but the unless block is executed when the expression is nil or false. Take a look at the unless version:

```
pattern_matching/lib/elixir_flows/unless/number_compare.ex
defmodule NumberCompareWithUnless do
  def greater(number, other_number) do
    unless number < other_number do
      number
    else
      other_number
    end
  end
end
```

Using unless and else in the same expression makes it very hard to understand at first. It's good to avoid creating expressions like this; use if instead.

if and unless are expressions that return the resulting value of the executed code block. The else block is optional and the expression returns nil when the condition is falsy in an omitted else.

case, cond, if, and unless are control-flow structures built with macro functions. You can invoke them using the function-invocation syntax. In the following example, you can see how to invoke the if control flow like a function:

```
if(number >= other_number, do: number, else: other_number)
```

The Elixir control-flow structures solve common problems by determining which expressions should be executed. But be careful: creating too many functions to control flow can sometimes damage your code health with unnecessary indirection. When you overuse Elixir's built-in control-flow structures, such as if, your code will look more imperative than functional. To program with functional thinking, your code should express *what* it needs to do, and that means balancing the use of control-flow features and function clauses.

## Wrapping Up

This has been an eye-opening chapter. You'll never look at equals signs and function arguments the same. Pattern matching is an excellent feature; once you take the first step, you won't go back. Let's see what we've explored:

- We can use pattern matching in simple variable assignments.

- The = operator lets us create a pattern-matching expression that makes two things match, or fail if there's no match.

- Pattern matching can extract values of complex data types in a process called destructuring.

- Function clauses and pattern matching can help us control the program flow.

- We can use Elixir control-flow structures to solve simple tasks quickly.

Knowing how to control the program flow opens up the possibility of learning how to repeat and stop program tasks to solve various problems. In the next chapter you'll learn that in a functional way, using function recursion.

## Your Turn

- In RPGs, players have points to spend on their character attributes. Create a function that returns the total number of points players have spent on their characters. The function will receive a map containing the strength, dexterity, and intelligence values. Each point in strength should be multiplied by two, and dexterity and intelligence should be multiplied by three.

- Create a function that returns Tic-Tac-Toe game winners. You can represent the board with a list of nine elements, where each group of three items is a row. The return of the function should be a tuple. When we have a winner, the first element should be the atom :winner, and the second should be the player. When we have no winner, the tuple should contain one item that is the atom :no_winner. It should work like this:

```
TicTacToe.winner({
  :x, :o, :x,
  :o, :x, :o,
  :o, :o, :x
})
# {:winner, :x}

TicTacToe.winner({
  :x, :o, :x,
  :o, :x, :o,
  :o, :x, :o
})
# :no_winner
```

- Create a function that calculates income tax following these rules: a salary equal or below $2,000 pays no tax; below or equal to $3,000 pays 5%; below or equal to $6,000 pays 10%; everything higher than $6,000 pays 15%.

- Create an Elixir script where users can type their salary and see the income tax and the net wage. You can use the module from the previous exercise, but this script should parse the user input and display a message when users type something that is not a valid number.

# CHAPTER 4

# Diving into Recursion

A simple script that counts to 10, a homepage that shows recent news, a program that parses each line of a CSV file. What do these programs have in common? They all need to do repetitive tasks to determine the final result. Recursive functions are the core of repetition in functional programming.

In imperative languages, the repetition is done using iterative features like for and while loops, which rely on mutable state. In functional programming, we have the immutable state, so we need a different approach. Here we use recursive functions.

A recursive function is when a function calls itself, leading to successive calls of the same function. In this chapter, we'll look at strategies to work with recursion and avoid common pitfalls of performance and infinite processing. By the end of the chapter, we'll see how to work with recursion in lambda expressions. Our first step is to learn the most common type of recursion: the bounded recursion.

## Surrounded by Boundaries

A *bounded recursion* is a type of recursive function in which the successive calls to itself have an end. It's the most common type of recursive function, present in all list-navigation code. Every time a recursive function calls itself, that's an iteration; every time a bounded recursion iterates, it requires fewer iterations to finish. We're diminishing the steps to finish the program execution in each iteration, even if we can't easily predict the total number of iterations.

The number of repetitions of a bounded recursive function is directly associated with the arguments that it receives. We can see how it works by creating a program that sums all integers from 0 up to a parameterized number. For example, if we pass the number 3, the program will generate the sum 3 + 2 + 1 + 0. It must repeat the task of adding the resulting number and decrementing the given number by 1 until the given number reaches 0. If we pass a bigger number, the number of repetitions increases. Let's create this with a Sum module:

recursion/lib/sum.ex
```
defmodule Sum do
  def up_to(0), do: 0
  def up_to(n), do: n + up_to(n - 1)
end
```

And let's run it using IEx:

```
iex> c("sum.ex")
iex> Sum.up_to(10)
55
```

We've created two function clauses for the up_to/1 function. The first clause is executed when the argument matches 0, and it returns the number 0—nothing more. It's our stop condition, and the returning value is the last step of a series of repetitions. The other clause is the expression that will be repeated. You can notice it because it calls the up_to function, decrementing the number until it reaches the stop-condition clause. It receives a variable n, then sums the numbers using the current value of n and calls the same function by decreasing n by 1. Let's see how it works step by step:

```
up_to(5)
= 5 + up_to(4)
= 5 + 4 + up_to(3)
= 5 + 4 + 3 + up_to(2)
= 5 + 4 + 3 + 2 + up_to(1)
= 5 + 4 + 3 + 2 + 1 + up_to(0)
= 5 + 4 + 3 + 2 + 1 + 0
= 15
```

Recursion works by calling the same function again and again, repeating tasks until it reaches the clause that protects it from an infinite repetition. The boundary clause is very important; it should *always* be defined before the clauses that can be repeated. If we remove or swap the up_to(0) clause, it won't have a stop condition, and it will consume your machine resources forever, or until you kill the process or turn off the computer. If you want to feel the sensation of the infinite loop, you can remove or swap the boundary clause, compile the module again, and run the same example in your IEx. Be prepared to kill the process: you can use Ctrl+C twice in IEx to halt the execution and exit.

## Navigating Through Lists

Many programming tasks require you to work with lists, show database records, or parse each line of a file. These are a few examples of a broad range of tasks that use lists. They all are based on navigating through lists and doing some computation for each item. We can use the list syntax [head | tail] to navigate through the list elements using recursive functions. Let's see how we can work with lists by building a program that sums all the numbers of a collection. Let's build a sum function that does this job for us:

recursion/lib/math.ex
```elixir
defmodule Math do
  def sum([]), do: 0
  def sum([head | tail]), do: head + sum(tail)
end
```

We can run it using IEx:

```
iex> c("math.ex")
iex> Math.sum([10, 5, 15])
30
iex> Math.sum([])
0
```

First let's look at the recursive function clause. [head | tail] extracts the first number to the variable head, and the rest of the elements in the list to the variable tail. Then we use the + operator to sum the first number with a recursive call of sum, passing the rest of the list. It repeats—decreasing the number of items in each new call of sum—until it reaches the boundary clause that matches an empty list. The clause sum([]) is the stop condition, and it says that the sum of an empty list is 0. Let's look at how it works step by step:

```
sum([10, 5, 15]])
= 10 + sum([5, 15])
= 10 + 5 + sum([15])
= 10 + 5 + 15 + sum([])
= 10 + 5 + 15 + 0
= 30
```

The function sum is called, and it generates a new sum call. For each iteration, the number of elements of the list decreases until the list is empty. With the same logic, we can use recursive functions to navigate through any data structure. We only need to know how to reduce the data for the next iterations and identify when the data reaches the stop condition.

## Transforming Lists

In daily programming, we often face situations in which we need to transform things into other things. Lists are the main actors in the routine of data transformations. Examples include transforming: debit accounts into blocked accounts, draft blog posts into published posts, strings into data structures, and user inputs into table rows. Data is immutable in functional programming, so when we transform data, we're building new data. The process of transformation in lists requires repetitive steps, and we can use recursive functions to do it. Let's see how we can build new lists using recursion in Elixir.

The [head | tail] syntax is useful for destructuring arguments, but it's also useful for constructing new lists. Try the following code in your IEx to see how it works:

```
iex> [:a | [:b, :c]]
[:a, :b, :c]
iex> [:a, :b | [:c]]
[:a, :b, :c]
iex> [:a, :b, :c]
[:a, :b, :c]
```

Using that syntax, the expressions [:a | [:b, :c]] and [:a, :b | [:c]] result in the same list [:a, :b, :c]. With that in mind, we can use the same syntax to build a new list, transforming one element at a time. Note: Using this syntax, we're prepending an element to a list, which is many times faster than appending with the ++ operator. Let's see how we can use recursive functions to build an example in which we need to transform a list.

For this example, we'll travel to a fantasy world where magic and dragons are real. Edwin is a wizard who has a shop that sells magic items. His work—as an enchanter and a businessperson—is to transform regular items into magic items and apply a new selling price. Every item he enchants gets his name in its title. The selling price of an enchanted item is the original price multiplied by three. Let's build a module for this process of enchantment and sales preparation. Create a module called EnchanterShop in a file called enchanter_shop.ex. First, let's create a function with test data to understand how it's structured:

```
recursion/lib/enchanter_shop.ex
def test_data do
  [
    %{title: "Longsword", price: 50, magic: false},
    %{title: "Healing Potion", price: 60, magic: true},
    %{title: "Rope", price: 10, magic: false},
    %{title: "Dragon's Spear", price: 100, magic: true},
  ]
end
```

The items are a map structure. They have the item's title and price, and a flag saying whether the item is magic. Now we need to create the code that navigates through this list and makes the transformation. Let's create the enchant_for_sale function:

```
recursion/lib/enchanter_shop.ex
@enchanter_name "Edwin"

def enchant_for_sale([]), do: []
def enchant_for_sale([item | incoming_items]) do
  new_item = %{
    title: "#{@enchanter_name}'s #{item.title}",
    price: item.price * 3,
    magic: true
  }

  [new_item | enchant_for_sale(incoming_items)]
end
```

The first function clause is for when the list of products is empty, which results in an empty list of items for sale. The check clause for empty lists is also the stop condition for the list navigation. The second clause is where the recursive transformation happens. We use pattern matching to extract the first item, and then we create a new magic item by applying the transformation rules. The item's title now receives the enchanter's name, the price is tripled, and the magic flag is true. Then in the last expression, we build a new list using the [head | tail] syntax, where the first element is a new item transformed, and the rest of the list is a recursive call of enchant_for_sale.

> ## The Key-based Accessors
>
> In Elixir, keywords and maps have a syntax to access values by using keys in []. If the key is missing, a nil value is returned and no error is raised.
>
> ```
> item = %{magic: true, price: 150, title: "Edwin's Longsword"}
> item[:title] # returns "Edwin's Longsword"
> item["owner"] # returns nil
> item[:creator][:city] # returns nil
> ```
>
> Elixir also provides key-based accessors for structs and maps to access values associated with atom keys using dot notation. If the key is missing, an error is raised.
>
> ```
> item = %{magic: true, price: 150, title: "Edwin's Longsword"}
> item.title # returns "Edwin's Longsword"
> item.owner # raises a KeyError
> ```
>
> You can learn more about key-based accessors from the Elixir official documentation.[a]
>
> ---
>
> a.    https://hexdocs.pm/elixir/Access.html

Let's see how it works using IEx:

```
iex> c("enchanter_shop.ex")
iex> EnchanterShop.enchant_for_sale(EnchanterShop.test_data)
[%{magic: true, price: 150, title: "Edwin's Longsword"},
 %{magic: true, price: 180, title: "Edwin's Healing Potion"},
 %{magic: true, price: 30, title: "Edwin's Rope"},
 %{magic: true, price: 300, title: "Edwin's Dragon's Spear"}]
```

We have done the transformation. Now the simple longsword is the magical and awesome *Edwin's Longsword*. But wait a moment. Some of the items in the list were already magical. We cannot enchant something that is already enchanted.

Let's fix our code by applying a clause that won't do a transformation when the item is already magical. Let's put the new clause between the stop condition and the transformation clause:

```
recursion/lib/enchanter_shop.ex
def enchant_for_sale([]), do: []
➤ def enchant_for_sale([item = %{magic: true} | incoming_items]) do
➤   [item | enchant_for_sale(incoming_items)]
➤ end
def enchant_for_sale([item | incoming_items]) do
  new_item = %{
    title: "#{@enchanter_name}'s #{item.title}",
    price: item.price * 3,
    magic: true
  }

  [new_item | enchant_for_sale(incoming_items)]
end
```

In the filter function clause, we check if an item is magical by using map pattern matching. We check if the argument contains the subset %{magic: true}. When it matches, we bind the map parameter to the variable item. Then we don't do any item transformation; instead, we build a list where the first element is the same item, and the rest of the list is a recursive call to enchant_for_sale.

We can compile it again and see the filter in action:

```
iex> c("enchanter_shop.ex")
iex> EnchanterShop.enchant_for_sale(EnchanterShop.test_data)
[%{magic: true, price: 150, title: "Edwin's Longsword"},
 %{magic: true, price: 60, title: "Healing Potion"},
 %{magic: true, price: 30, title: "Edwin's Rope"},
 %{magic: true, price: 100, title: "Dragon's Spear"}]
```

This time, the Healing Potion and the Dragon's Spear keep their original attributes since they were already magical. With this module, we have seen how to transform lists and how to use function clauses to skip unnecessary transformations.

# Conquering Recursion

For many developers, recursive functions are one of the hardest things to understand when moving to functional programming. Finding the stop-condition clause and making the function call itself can be confusing. Functional programmers work more with recursive functions than developers in other paradigms, because recursive functions are the core of code repetition. If you want to become a functional programmer, it's important that you don't get stuck every time you face a recursive function.

There are two helpful techniques for solving problems using recursive functions: *decrease and conquer* and *divide and conquer*. We'll explore them next.

## Decrease and Conquer

Decrease and conquer is a technique for reducing a problem to its simplest form and starting to solve it incrementally. By doing this, we find the most obvious solution to a tiny part of the problem. From there we start to *conquer* progressively, incrementing the problem step by step. Let's experiment with this approach using a well-known problem: the factorial.

The factorial of a number is the product of all positive integers less than or equal to it. If we want to know the factorial of 3, we use the 3 * 2 * 1 expression. Using the decrease-and-conquer strategy, the first step is to find the *base case*, the simplest factorial scenario. We'll use the base case to help solve more complex ones. Let's write it in a module, expecting a number from 0 to 4:

recursion/lib/factorial.ex
```
defmodule Factorial do
  def of(0), do: 1
  def of(1), do: 1
  def of(2), do: 2 * 1
  def of(3), do: 3 * 2 * 1
  def of(4), do: 4 * 3 * 2 * 1
end
```

The factorial for the number 4 is 4 * 3 * 2 * 1. For the number 3, it's 3 * 2 * 1, and so on until we find the solution. The base scenario for the factorial is when the argument is 0 or 1. We can't keep going because a factorial works only with positive numbers. We don't need calculations for 0 and 1 because the result is 1. We can compile the code and try what we have done using IEx:

```
iex> c("factorial.ex")
iex> Factorial.of(0)
1
iex> Factorial.of(1)
1
iex> Factorial.of(4)
24
iex> Factorial.of(5)
** (FunctionClauseError) no function clause matching in Factorial.of/1
iex> Factorial.of(-1)
** (FunctionClauseError) no function clause matching in Factorial.of/1
```

We can't just take the biggest factorial number we want to calculate and write all the functions until we reach it. Let's take a closer look at the factorial of 3. With the expression 3 * 2 * 1, we can write it as 3 * (2 * 1) and it returns the same result. The expression (2 * 1) is the same body as the factorial of 2. Then, instead of writing (2 * 1), we can use a recursive function call. Let's rewrite this function, replacing the calculations with function calls:

recursion/lib/factorial.ex
```
defmodule Factorial do
  def of(0), do: 1
  def of(1), do: 1 * of(0)
  def of(2), do: 2 * of(1)
  def of(3), do: 3 * of(2)
  def of(4), do: 4 * of(3)
end
```

We're almost there. Now the pattern for the solution of the factorial is clear. For a given number, we multiply it with the solution of the factorial of the previous number. That's how we *conquer* the problem. Let's now rewrite these functions to apply the pattern we've discovered:

recursion/lib/factorial.ex
```
defmodule Factorial do
  def of(0), do: 1
  def of(n) when n > 0, do: n * of(n - 1)
end
```

We're done! We've created the solution for the factorial problem using recursion. We've used the guard clause n > 0 to ensure that only numbers greater than our base clause are permitted. That's how to use the decrease-and-conquer approach: First reduce the problem to find its base clause, then look out for the recursive call pattern in the problem we've reduced.

## Divide and Conquer

The divide-and-conquer technique is about separating the problem into two or more parts that can be processed independently and can be combined in the end. This technique is not only useful for recursive algorithms; it helps with many other tasks in programming. For example, imagine that we need to build a news homepage that will contain the most recent articles, headlines, and sports and culture sections. If we try to fetch all this content from the database at once, the SELECT query would be hard to write and maintain. The best approach is to *divide* the query into smaller independent operations for each desired piece of content. Then, in the end, we can combine all the results from the database and *conquer* the solution of the news homepage. We can use the same approach with recursive functions. Let's experiment by creating a function that sorts a list.

Sorting functions are useful for displaying ascending or descending content, for creating a better visual experience for users, and for improving search algorithms. We want to build a function that receives a list and returns a list with items in ascending order. In functional programming, the data is immutable; we can't change the order of the values in a list. Instead, we need to build a new list. In the process of generating a new list, we must guarantee that it's sorted. Thinking about a function that does it all at once is hard; instead, we can *divide* the list in half. Now we have two lists to sort, but they're small. If we keep dividing, we'll end up with lists that each contain one element. Lists with one element are sorted! Then we need to merge these lists in a sorted way to finish the algorithm.

That's enough theory. Let's write our sorting function. First we need to learn how to divide a list in half. In Elixir the Enum.split/2 function generates two lists from one, splitting the items. Let's try it in an IEx session:

```
iex> Enum.split([:a, :b, :c], 1)
{[:a], [:b, :c]}
iex> Enum.split([:a, :b, :c], 2)
{[:a, :b], [:c]}
iex> Enum.split([:a, :b, :c], 3)
{[:a, :b, :c], []}
```

The Enum.split/2 returns a tuple with two lists, where the first list contains the number of elements that we specified in the function call. The rest of the list items go in the second list. To split it in half, we need to pass the median number of elements of a list. We'll use the Elixir function Enum.count/1 to calculate the total, and then divide it by two. Try it in your IEx:

```
iex> Enum.count([:a, :b, :c])
3
iex> Enum.count([:a, :b, :c, :d]) / 2
2.0
iex> Enum.count([:a, :b, :c]) / 2
1.5
```

It's a problem when the number of elements in a list is odd, because we can't pass floats to the split function or it will generate an error. We need an integer division here. We can do it using the Elixir Kernel.div/2 function. Try it:

```
iex> div(3, 2)
1
iex> div(4, 2)
2
```

Now we can combine all these functions to divide a list in half recursively. It's the first step in our sorting algorithm; the second step is to build a new list in a sorted way. Let's create the sorting function and put it in a Sort module. Type the following code in your sort.ex file:

recursion/lib/sort.ex
```
defmodule Sort do
  def ascending([]), do: []
  def ascending([a]), do: [a]
  def ascending(list) do
    half_size = div(Enum.count(list), 2)
    {list_a, list_b} = Enum.split(list, half_size)
    # We need to sort list_a and list_b
    # ascending(list_a)
    # ascending(list_b)
    # And merge them using some strategy
  end
end
```

We created an ascending function that only splits the lists, but will soon sort the elements. We created the stop-condition clauses for empty lists and lists containing one element by using pattern matching in the function argument. For lists with more than one item, we created a function clause that will divide it in two. We've used some Elixir built-in functions, such as Enum.split/2 and Enum.count/1, to help us focus on the sorting algorithm and not on list operations.

We divided the lists until they reached one element. Now we need to use these one-item lists to build a new sorted list. We need a merge function that will unify two lists by putting the smallest elements at the beginning of the list. This way, if we try to merge [9] and [5], the result will be [5, 9]. Since the arguments are sorted lists, we know that the first elements are the smallest.

Then we can extract the first item from both lists, compare them, and put the lower value in a new list. If we try to combine [5, 9] with [1, 2], it will be [1, 2, 5, 9]. Doing it recursively, we'll generate a sorted list in the end. Let's see how it works when merging [5, 9] and [1, 4, 5]:

```
merge([5, 9], [1, 4, 5])
[1 | merge([5, 9], [4, 5])]
[1, 4 | merge([5, 9], [5])]
[1, 4, 5 | merge([9], [5])]
[1, 4, 5, 5 | merge([9], [])]
[1, 4, 5, 5, 9]
```

Let's write the merge function that does this work for us:

recursion/lib/sort.ex
```
defp merge([], list_b), do: list_b
defp merge(list_a, []), do: list_a
defp merge([head_a | tail_a], list_b = [head_b | _]) when head_a <= head_b do
  [head_a | merge(tail_a, list_b)]
end
defp merge(list_a = [head_a | _], [head_b | tail_b]) when head_a > head_b do
  [head_b | merge(list_a, tail_b)]
end
```

The first two clauses are straightforward. If we try to merge an empty list with any other list, the result will be that other list. The clause head_a <= head_b means the first element of list_a is the smallest. Then we extract the first element of list_a and put it in the first spot in the new list using the expression [head_a | merge(tail_a, list_b)]. For the rest of the elements of the new list, we call merge recursively, passing the rest of the elements of the list a and passing the entire list_b. The clause head_a > head_b does the inverse operation, extracting and putting the first element of list_b in the new list's first spot.

Using the merge/2 function, we can now combine all the lists we've divided and build a new one. Let's add this call in our ascending function:

recursion/lib/sort.ex
```
def ascending([]), do: []
def ascending([a]), do: [a]
def ascending(list) do
  half_size = div(Enum.count(list), 2)
  {list_a, list_b} = Enum.split(list, half_size)
➤   merge(
➤     ascending(list_a),
➤     ascending(list_b)
➤   )
end
```

Before we pass the lists to the merge/2 function, we must ensure that lists are sorted. That's why we do a recursive call to the ascending function before the merge. It will recursively merge the divided lists like this:

```
merge(merge([9], [5]), merge(merge([1], [5]), [4]))
merge([5, 9], merge([1, 5], [4]))
merge([5, 9], [1, 4, 5])
[1, 4, 5, 5, 9]
```

In this sorting function, the recursive call for ascending can work independently; all the recursive calls are not connected with each other. For example, we can compute them in parallel, although in the end we need to join both results to present a sorted list using the merge function. We can try our Sort module using IEx:

```
iex> c("sort.ex")
iex> Sort.ascending([9, 5, 1, 5, 4])
[1, 4, 5, 5, 9]
iex> Sort.ascending([2, 2, 3, 1])
[1, 2, 2, 3]
iex> Sort.ascending(["c", "d", "a", "c"])
["a", "c", "c", "d"]
```

We did it! The sorting algorithm is working. This algorithm is known as the *merge sort*.[1] It's one of the most famous divide-and-conquer algorithms.

Divide and conquer, as you may have noticed, is very similar to decrease and conquer. The main difference is that while the *decrease* strategy is focused on reducing the problem until we find a base clause, the *divide* technique is about separating the problem into two or more parts. These parts can be processed independently and be combined in the end. As you can see, recursion does a lot of function calls and it may cause performance bottlenecks. In the next section you'll learn how create recursive functions that use your machine resources prudently.

## Tail-Call Optimization

Every time we call a function, it consumes memory. Usually we don't need to worry much about it—machines today have plenty of memory, and the Erlang VM does a great job keeping computation costs low for a decent amount of data. But when some input makes our function do millions of recursive calls, that consumes significant memory. In this section, we'll discuss a way of creating recursive functions that have constant and low memory consumption. We'll take advantage of compiler *tail-call optimization*.

---

1. https://en.wikipedia.org/wiki/Merge_sort

Tail-call optimization is when the compiler reduces functions in memory without allocating more memory. It's a common compiler feature in functional programming languages. To use it, we need to ensure that the last expression of our function is a function call. If the last expression is a new function call, then the current function's return is the return of the new function call and it doesn't need to keep the current function in memory. Consider this example:

```
iex> scream = fn word -> String.upcase("#{word}!!!") end
iex> scream.("help")
"HELP!!!!"
```

When we invoke scream.("help") the program will put it in the memory stack and then execute the function's body. The scream function will interpolate the word *help* and that will result in "help!!!". The last expression will result in a function call like this: String.upcase("help!!!"). This means the result of scream.("help") is the same as String.upcase("help!!!"). Finally, the program will optimize the memory by removing scream.("help") from the function call stack.

Let's take another look at the recursive part of our Factorial module:

recursion/lib/factorial.ex
```
def of(n) when n > 0, do: n * of(n - 1)
```

We have a recursive call on the last line, but the last expression is a call to the * operator. Elixir will execute the of(n - 1) call and use the result to calculate the n * expression. This function is a body-recursive function—one in which the last expression isn't a recursive call—and it's impossible take advantage of the tail-call optimization. We can simulate the memory problem that body-recursive function may face by using a big number to generate millions of recursive calls. You can use a process monitor to see the huge impact it will create in memory. Be ready to kill the process, because it will take a long time to finish. Try it in your IEx:

```
iex> c("factorial.ex")
iex> Factorial.of(10_000_000)
```

Here's what I measured when I did this experiment:

You may see a different memory-consumption number on your machine, but it will be very high. It takes a lot of memory to do repetitive tasks. We can improve this by transforming that function into a *tail-recursive* function—a function that has a recursive call in the last expression.

The common approach to creating tail-recursive functions is to replace the use of the function result with an extra argument that accumulates the results of each iteration. Let's create a tail-recursive version of the Factorial module and compare it to the previous version. Let's create a module called TRFactorial:

```
recursion/lib/tr_factorial.ex
defmodule TRFactorial do
  def of(n), do: factorial_of(n, 1)
  defp factorial_of(0, acc), do: acc
  defp factorial_of(n, acc) when n > 0, do: factorial_of(n - 1, n * acc)
end
```

We've created a factorial_of helper function that will have the extra argument for accumulating the multiplications. The argument acc has the result of the previous iteration. When we do the recursive call, we pass the result with the expression acc * n. The last expression is a recursive call, not a call to the * operator. Now the function is tail-recursive and can be optimized by the compiler. We can try this new version using IEx and measure the memory consumption. Be ready to stop the execution, because even with the memory optimization it will take a long time to finish.

```
iex> c("tr_factorial.ex")
iex> TRFactorial.of(10_000_000)
```

Here's what I measured on my machine:

That's a huge improvement! However, at the same time we made our code a bit more complex. It's a serious trade-off that we need to think about before deciding if we should write a body-recursive or a tail-recursive function. In general, if you're expecting millions of iterations or the tail-recursive function isn't hard to read and maintain, go with tail-recursive. If the number of iterations is small and the tail-recursive function is hard to understand and maintain, go with body-recursive.

# Functions Without Borders

*Unbounded* recursion is when we can't predict the number of repetitions for a recursive function. For example, it's hard to predict how many iterations a web crawler that navigates and downloads web pages will have. For each page it browses, it finds new links to crawl. Since we're not the owners of the pages, we can't predict how many links each page will have. For every page the crawler downloads, the list of pages that needs to be crawled can increase. The web crawler also needs to be cautious with pages it has already visited so it avoids circular references and infinite recursion. All these characteristics of the web crawler represent unbounded recursion challenges, and a functional programmer must be prepared to face them. The following image illustrates the nature of data that leads to an unbounded recursion.

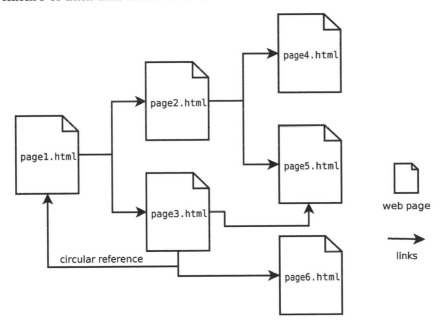

We're not necessarily reducing the problem with each step, and we can't predict how many steps will be required to finish. A similar problem occurs when software tries to map a machine's file system, even if it's a more controlled environment than the web. Each directory it finds can have many more directories inside. Let's explore this type of recursion, creating a program that prints and navigates through a given system directory. Create a module called Navigator:

```
recursion/lib/navigator.ex
defmodule Navigator do
  def navigate(dir) do
    expanded_dir = Path.expand(dir)
    go_through([expanded_dir])
  end

  defp go_through([]), do: nil
  defp go_through([content | rest]) do
    print_and_navigate(content, File.dir?(content))
    go_through(rest)
  end

  defp print_and_navigate(_dir, false), do: nil
  defp print_and_navigate(dir, true) do
    IO.puts dir
    children_dirs = File.ls!(dir)
    go_through(expand_dirs(children_dirs, dir))
  end

  defp expand_dirs([], _relative_to), do: []
  defp expand_dirs([dir | dirs], relative_to) do
    expanded_dir = Path.expand(dir, relative_to)
    [expanded_dir | expand_dirs(dirs, relative_to)]
  end
end
```

The function navigate is our entry point. For example, we can pass .., which Path.expand/1 will transform into a complete path. Then we call the go_through helper, passing the directory in a list. Let's see this function in detail:

```
recursion/lib/navigator.ex
defp go_through([]), do: nil
defp go_through([content | rest]) do
  print_and_navigate(content, File.dir?(content))
  go_through(rest)
end
```

In the go_through/1 function we have a stop clause for an empty directory and another clause that navigates through the contents of that directory. For each piece of content, we try to print its path and navigate through its children. After that, we do a recursive call to keep navigating through the directory contents. Let's see print_and_navigate/2 in detail:

```
recursion/lib/navigator.ex
defp print_and_navigate(_dir, false), do: nil
defp print_and_navigate(dir, true) do
  IO.puts dir
  children_dirs = File.ls!(dir)
  go_through(expand_dirs(children_dirs, dir))
end
```

This function's clause checks the directory flag. It stops the iteration when it encounters something that's not a directory. Otherwise, it lists all the contents using the File.ls!/1. The function that lists the directory contents returns only the name of the files and directories. To check if something is a directory, we need the full path of that directory. Then we use our custom function expand_dirs/2 to transform it. With the full path in hand, we can discover its contents using the function go_through/1. This can take a long time. Be ready to stop the execution if you don't want to wait. Let's try it using IEx:

```
iex> c("navigator.ex")
iex> Navigator.navigate("../..")
```

This example tries to navigate in two directories above the current one. Each machine has a different structure, and the output and duration can be very different. To create more predictable functions, let's write some code to reduce the number of iterations. We'll explore two strategies—one that focuses on limiting the number of iterations and another that focuses on avoiding infinite loops.

## Adding Boundaries

Now our navigator can dive into the directory children, the children of children, and so on. We can create a stop condition that interrupts our unbounded function and keeps it from running too long. We can add any restriction that we think is appropriate. For example, it could be a timer that stops the process after two minutes, or stops after accumulating a number of results. We can be more accurate about when the function finishes, adding one or more restrictions. Let's experiment by creating a stop condition for our directory navigator, and let's add a limit to how deep it can dive.

We'll add a *depth* restriction that will flag how many child directories deep we want to dive from the given directory. For example, given a depth of two and the directory root, we'll navigate only as deep as root/children/children. It considerably reduces the scope of navigation, and our recursion will be more predictable. Let's see in each step how to add the depth restriction. First, we need to store a value indicating how deep we can dive. Let's create a module attribute for it:

```
recursion/lib/depth_navigator.ex
@max_depth 2
```

Now we need to start our navigation using an initial value. In our entry-point function navigate, we can pass the initial value 0:

recursion/lib/depth_navigator.ex
```
def navigate(dir) do
  expanded_dir = Path.expand(dir)
  go_through([expanded_dir], 0)
end
```

Now we need to change our print_and_navigate function to accept a third argument. Then every time we navigate into a child directory, we can increment the current depth value. Let's see how:

recursion/lib/depth_navigator.ex
```
defp print_and_navigate(_dir, false, _current_depth), do: nil
defp print_and_navigate(dir, true, current_depth) do
  IO.puts dir
  children_dirs = File.ls!(dir)
  go_through(expand_dirs(children_dirs, dir), current_depth + 1)
end
```

Now that we're incrementing the depth value, we need to create a stop condition. We must change our go_through function to accept the current depth argument. In the go_through definition, we can add a clause that will prevent the navigation when the current depth is greater than the maximum depth:

recursion/lib/depth_navigator.ex
```
defp go_through([], _current_depth), do: nil
defp go_through(_dirs, current_depth) when current_depth > @max_depth, do: nil
defp go_through([content | rest], current_depth) do
  print_and_navigate(content, File.dir?(content), current_depth)
  go_through(rest, current_depth)
end
```

That's it. We've added a restriction to control the number of repetitions for our recursive function. The previous version was unpredictable because its only condition was when the directories had no children. With this new version, our function interactions are more controlled because there's an additional stop condition that ends the iterations after a certain number of nesting directories.

## Avoiding Infinite Loops

Depending on the problem you're solving, your recursion algorithm can fall into an infinite loop and the program will run indefinitely. For example, when a web crawler is navigating through pages it needs to extract links to visit more pages. If it extracts links of a previously visited page, it will visit that page again and extract more visited pages, starting an infinite loop. That infinite loop is caused by a circular reference in the pages. There are various strategies to detect and avoid circular references. You must find the one that fits best for your problem. In the web-crawler example, we can store all the visited URLs and check them before visiting a new page. In our directory-navigator example, we may face the same web-crawler problem when our operating system has symbolic-links support. Let's explore how to avoid unnecessary iterations by detecting directories with symbolic links.

As illustrated in the following figure, a symbolic link is when you create a directory that's a link to another directory in the system. It works like a portal: if you go through it, you reach the other directory's contents. If we have a directory that contains a link for a parent directory, we have a circular reference. Navigating through it will lead us into an infinite loop.

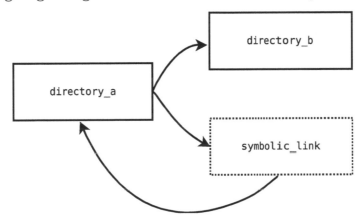

One way to solve this problem in our file-system navigator is by checking if the directory is a real directory and not a symbolic link. We can use File.lstat/1 to get the content type. Passing a path, it returns a File.Stat struct that contains the attribute type with an atom value. When the content is a directory, it returns :directory. When it's a symbolic link, it returns :symlink. We can create our custom _dir? function to navigate only when something is a real directory.

recursion/lib/slink_skip_navigator.ex
```
def dir?(dir) do
  {:ok, %{type: type}} = File.lstat(dir)
  type == :directory
end
```

With this function, we can replace all the File.dir? calls to our custom function. It ensures that our navigator will not follow symbolic links, avoiding falling into a circular reference. Avoiding symbolic links isn't a perfect solution because for some use cases it might be useful to navigate into symbolic links. Dealing with unbounded recursions isn't easy, as it requires tests and an incremental improvement to find a solution for your scenario.

## Using Recursion with Anonymous Functions

We've created and practiced many examples using recursion and named functions. When we create recursive functions, we call functions that have the same name of the function that we're creating, and it has been working great. The compiler knows how to use that function-name reference to call the function that we creating. It's very practical! But in the world of anonymous functions, it's not that easy—we face problems in the anonymous functions' definition. Let's see the problems in action, creating the factorial example using anonymous functions:

```
iex> factorial = fn
  0 -> 1
  x when x > 0 -> x * factorial.(x - 1)
end
** (CompileError) undefined function factorial/0
```

We can't do a recursive call to the factorial function because that variable isn't created yet. To use it, we need it to have been created previously. What a dilemma! We need to create something that requires itself to have already been created. We can solve this problem by wrapping the function in another function and delaying recursive call execution. First we need to create a reference for the function itself in the argument. To avoid the problem of the nonexistent function error, we can delay the function evaluation, wrapping it inside of another function. Here's how:

```
iex> fact_gen = fn me ->
  fn
    0 -> 1
    x when x > 0 -> x * me.(me).(x - 1)
  end
end
iex> factorial = fact_gen.(fact_gen)
iex> factorial.(5)
120
iex> factorial.(10)
3628800
```

It works! Let's review it step by step. We created a function called fact_gen that knows how to build a factorial function and expect itself to be passed in as an argument. Then, the me argument represents the factorial generator, representing itself. We can't call it by directly passing a number to me since it's a factorial creator and the first argument must be a reference to itself. So, to produce the factorial function we use the expression me.(me). With the function built, we can finally call it, passing the number argument. Then the expression factorial = fact_gen.(fact_gen) generates our factorial to be used with numbers. The problem here is that me.(me) is not expressive; it doesn't look like the factorial definition. Code must be expressive to be easier to maintain. Recursion with anonymous functions isn't straightforward, but is possible. In Elixir, we can use the capturing feature to use named-function references like anonymous functions:

```
iex> c("factorial.ex")
iex> factorial = &Factorial.of/1
iex> factorial.(5)
120
```

We explored the capturing operator in detail in *Using Named Functions as Values*, on page 29. The & operator captures a reference to a function, providing a beautiful way of using named functions as values. So if you need an anonymous recursive function, create a named function and use the & operator to capture the function's reference.

## Wrapping Up

We've reached the end of another chapter! You've learned that recursive functions are the core of repetition in functional programming. Recursion is a big subject. Let's see what we've covered:

- We created recursive functions to solve tasks that need repetition.

- We transformed a collection of data into a new one using recursion.

- We studied the *decrease-and-conquer* and *divide-and-conquer* strategies of solving problems.

- We saw how to avoid performance problems using tail-recursive functions.

- We covered strategies to work with unbounded recursion.

- We saw how named functions are simpler than anonymous functions when working with recursion.

With this knowledge, we can face almost any problem that requires a repetition task using functional programming. But the repetition subject isn't over yet! Despite recursion being a powerful technique, using it for all code that needs to repeat tasks requires a lot of function definitions. With this extra code, it's easy to make a mistake, like forgetting some stop condition, which can result in an infinite loop. We can improve the recursive code using powerful abstractions created with *higher-order functions*. We'll do that in the next chapter.

## Your Turn

- Write two recursive functions: one that finds the biggest element of a list and another that finds the smallest. You should use them like this:

```
MyList.max([4, 2, 16, 9, 10])
# => 16
MyList.min([4, 2, 16, 9, 10])
# => 2
```

- In the section *Transforming Lists*, on page 62, we traveled to a fantasy world and enchanted some items. Create a new module called GeneralStore where you can create a function that filters based on whether the products are magical. You can use the same test data from EnchanterShop:

```
GeneralStore.filter_items(GeneralStore.test_data, magic: true)
# => [%{title: "Healing Potion", price: 60, magic: true},
# %{title: "Dragon's Spear", price: 100, magic: true}]
GeneralStore.filter_items(GeneralStore.test_data, magic: false)
# => [%{title: "Longsword", price: 50, magic: false},
# %{title: "Rope", price: 10, magic: false}]
```

- We've created a function that sorts the items of a list in ascending order. Now create a Sort.descending/1 function that sorts the elements in descending order.

- We've written a lot of recursive functions, but not all of them are tail recursive. Write the tail-recursive versions of Sum.up_to/1 and Math.sum/1. Extra challenge: write the tail-recursive version of Sort.merge/2.

- In the section *Adding Boundaries*, on page 75, we added a depth restriction to limit how many directories deep our module should dive. Now create a BreadthNavigator module that has a breadth constraint; it will be the maximum number of sibling directories it can navigate.

# CHAPTER 5

# Using Higher-Order Functions

Higher-order functions are those that have functions in their arguments and/or can return functions. They are useful for hiding the complexity of tedious and laborious routines. Having functions in input and output enables developers to create simple interfaces to help other parts of the code focus on what matters. For example, let's try File.open/3 in an IEx session:

```
iex> File.open("file.txt", [:write], &(IO.write(&1, "Hello, World!")))
```

The last argument of File.open/3 is a function that receives the file device. We can write and read its contents using the IO module. The main benefit of using it in this way is we don't need to worry if the file will be closed, because it will. Another example of higher-order functions is spawning a process. Let's try it:

```
iex> spawn fn -> IO.puts "Hello, World!" end
```

The spawn starts a process and calls the given function. It hides all the hard work of allocating memory and making it available to some core of your CPU to execute. It provides a simple interface for us; we only need to worry what our function will do in the new process.

The primary purpose of the higher-order function is to provide a way to build better functions with simple interfaces. In this chapter, we'll explore how higher-order functions help to create reusable code, combine functions, and work with lazy computation. We'll use the & operator a lot to create short expressions to build and reference functions. If you don't remember it, refer back to *Using Named Functions as Values*, on page 29. Our first step will be to practice how to build higher-order functions.

## Creating Higher-Order Functions for Lists

Using functions in variables, like with any other value, can be hard to remember for newcomers. To practice, we'll work with a subject familiar to us: lists. They're a useful data type and are present in almost any program we need to build. We've seen how to work with them using recursive functions, but if we stop and look again at all that code we've written, we'll see that they are a little bit repetitive and boring. We always have code that navigates through each item, and a stop condition when the list is empty. It's time to change it! We'll look at how to build higher-order functions that hide the tedious tasks and provide an interface for what matters. Let's start with the navigation routine.

## Navigating Through Items of a List

A common task when working with lists is to travel through all the items and do some computation on them. The first higher-order function we'll create permits us to navigate a list by passing a function that will compute each item. Our first task is to create a variable that holds a list to test. Let's go back to our old fantasy friend Edwin and store some of his enchanted items in a variable. Open your IEx and type the code that will create the magic recipient:

```
iex> enchanted_items = [
  %{title: "Edwin's Longsword", price: 150},
  %{title: "Healing Potion", price: 60},
  %{title: "Edwin's Rope", price: 30},
  %{title: "Dragon's Spear", price: 100}
]
```

Now people are coming to the store and want to know the items' names. Let's create some code that prints that information. With this routine, Edwin can prepare more magic potions while the program states the items' names for the buyers. To do that, we need to navigate through each list element. In this chapter, we'll create several functions for lists, then create a module called MyList in a my_list.ex file and put all the functions there. The first function will be called each/2. Write the following code:

```
higher_order_functions/0/my_list.ex
defmodule MyList do
  def each([], _function), do: nil
  def each([head | tail], function) do
    function.(head)
    each(tail, function)
  end
end
```

The function receives two arguments: the first is the list that we'll navigate, and the second is a function that will be called, passing each element of the list. The stop-condition clause is called when the list is empty; then it does nothing. The other clause is called when the list has elements; then we use the code function.(head) to call the function received in the argument, passing an element of the list. It runs recursively when the list has multiple elements. Let's try it using our IEx:

```
iex> c("my_list.ex")
iex> MyList.each(enchanted_items, fn item -> IO.puts item.title end)
Edwin's Longsword
Healing Potion
Edwin's Rope
Dragon's Spear
```

We've used MyList.each/2 to navigate through each element of the list. The most interesting part is that when we use that function, we don't need to worry about stop conditions or recursion. All that complexity is hidden. We only need to pass the function that must be executed through each item. It's the same thing to say we have passed an *action* that will happen during the list navigation. We can use this function with different lists and change the result the way we like:

```
items = ["dogs", "cats", "flowers"]
iex> MyList.each(items, fn item -> IO.puts String.capitalize(item) end)
Dogs
Cats
Flowers
iex> MyList.each(items, fn item -> IO.puts String.upcase(item) end)
DOGS
CATS
FLOWERS
iex> MyList.each(items, fn item -> IO.puts String.length(item) end)
4
4
7
```

We've used the same collection and completed different tasks easily. It shows how higher-order functions are powerful for helping us reuse code and hide complexity.

## Transforming Lists

Let's practice more. Another common task is generating new lists. We can reduce the complexity of this generation by creating a higher-order function. Let's imagine that the town where Edwin sells his items has increased the sales tax rate; now he needs to increase the price of his items by 10% in order to make the same profit. We need to generate a new list with the new prices. Let's go back to our module MyList and add this new function:

```
higher_order_functions/my_list.ex
def map([], _function), do: []
def map([head | tail], function) do
  [function.(head) | map(tail, function)]
end
```

The MyList.map/2 that we have created receives two arguments. The first is the list that we'll navigate and the second is the function that we're going to pass each item to and use its return to build a new list. The stop-condition clause is when we have an empty list. The other clause uses the list syntax to make a new list. On the new list head, we have the returning value of the given function. That function receives the current list head. On the new list tail, we have a recursive call of the map function. We created a function that generates a new list by applying some computation on each item. The map name is an inheritance of mathematics terminology that means transforming a set to another one. Let's see it in action:

```
iex> c("my_list.ex")
iex> increase_price = fn i -> %{title: i.title, price: i.price * 1.1} end
iex> MyList.map(enchanted_items, increase_price)
[%{price: 165.0, title: "Edwin's Longsword"},
 %{price: 66.0, title: "Healing Potion"},
 %{price: 33.0, title: "Edwin's Rope"},
 %{price: 110.00000000000001, title: "Dragon's Spear"}]
```

You can simplify increase_price by using Elixir's built-in higher-order function Kernel.update_in/2 to update a map. Take a look:

```
iex> increase_price = fn item -> update_in(item.price, &(&1 * 1.1)) end
iex> MyList.map(enchanted_items, increase_price)
[%{price: 165.0, title: "Edwin's Longsword"},
 %{price: 66.0, title: "Healing Potion"},
 %{price: 33.0, title: "Edwin's Rope"},
 %{price: 110.00000000000001, title: "Dragon's Spear"}]
```

The update_in/2 function is useful for updating a map without having to write all the keys to build a new one. We can use our map/2 function to transform any list we want. Try it:

```
items = ["dogs", "cats", "flowers"]
iex> MyList.map(items, &String.capitalize/1)
["Dogs", "Cats", "Flowers"]
iex> MyList.map(items, &String.upcase/1)
["DOGS", "CATS", "FLOWERS"]
iex> MyList.map(["45.50", "32.12", "86.0"], &String.to_float/1)
[45.5, 32.12, 86.0]
```

When we use the map, the task of transforming lists becomes easier. All the work of iterating and building a new list is hidden; we only need to think about the transformation on each item.

## Reducing Lists to One Value

The next task is to create a function that transforms a list into one value. For example, it can be useful to discover how much income Edwin can have. To see it, we need to sum all his items' prices. Let's write a higher-order function that will make the job easier:

```
higher_order_functions/my_list.ex
def reduce([], acc, _function), do: acc
def reduce([head | tail], acc, function) do
  reduce(tail, function.(head, acc), function)
end
```

In the first argument, the MyList.reduce/3 function expects a list that will be navigated. The second parameter is an initial value to be accumulated during navigation. The third argument is a function that will be used to apply a computation on the list's item and the value accumulated, generating a new accumulated value. The first function clause is for empty lists. The second clause iterates recursively on each item, updating the accumulated value. Let's sum all of Edwin's items' prices using this function:

```
iex> c("my_list.ex")
iex> sum_price = fn item, sum -> item.price + sum end
iex> MyList.reduce(enchanted_items, 0, sum_price)
340
```

The initial value to accumulate the items' price is 0, then on each iteration reduce uses the sum_price function result to update the accumulated value. The sum_price function takes two parameters: the item of the list and the current accumulated value. We sum both values, and the result is the new accumulated value. We can use the reduce/3 function to work with any generic list we want. Try it:

```
iex> MyList.reduce([10, 5, 5, 10], 0, &+/2)
30
iex> MyList.reduce([5, 4, 3, 2, 1], 1, &*/2)
120
iex> MyList.reduce([100, 20, 400, 200], 100, &max/2)
400
iex> MyList.reduce([100, 20, 400, 200], 100, &min/2)
20
```

Using the reduce/3 function, we can focus only on the operation that accumulates the value. The work of iterating over each item by recursively updating accumulated values is hidden from us.

## Filtering Items of a List

The last function we'll build for lists is very common and useful: filtering a list by applying some criteria. Going back to Edwin's shop, let's imagine the customers want to see only the products that cost less than 70 gold coins. We need to filter the shop items by applying the criteria *price less than 70*. When we're filtering, we're creating a new list with only the elements that pass the criteria.

Let's create the following function that will filter the items for us:

```
higher_order_functions/my_list.ex
def filter([], _function), do: []
def filter([head | tail], function) do
  if function.(head) do
    [head | filter(tail, function)]
  else
    filter(tail, function)
  end
end
```

The MyList.filter/2 function calls the given criteria function by passing each list item. If it returns a *falsy* value, it means the item should not be on the new list. Everything that is *truthy*, not nil or false, means it has passed the criteria and should be in the new list. For truthy or falsy cases, the function will keep building the new list and make a recursive call on its tail. Let's see how much easier it is now to filter list items:

```
iex> c("my_list.ex")
iex> MyList.filter(enchanted_items, fn item -> item.price < 70 end)
[%{price: 60, title: "Healing Potion"}, %{price: 30, title: "Edwin's Rope"}]
```

Using our higher-order function filter/2, we just need to pass a function that checks if the item's price is less than 70 gold coins. We can use that function to filter any list. Try it:

```
iex> MyList.filter(["a", "b", "c", "d"], &(&1 > "b"))
["c", "d"]
iex> MyList.filter([100, 200, 300, 400], &(&1 < 300))
[100, 200]
iex> MyList.filter(["Alex", "Mike", "Ana"], &String.starts_with?(&1, "A"))
["Alex", "Ana"]
iex> MyList.filter(["a@b", "t.t", "a@b.c"], &String.contains?(&1, "@"))
["a@b", "a@b.c"]
```

When we use the filter/2 function, it's clear which data and filtering criteria we need to apply. All the complexity of navigating through lists, filtering, building new lists, and recursing is hidden from us.

## Using the Enum Module

The each, map, reduce, and filter list operations are useful. Almost all of the programming tasks you'll do with lists can benefit from these functions. Thanks to Elixir's core team, you don't need to write these higher-order functions every time you start a new Elixir project, because they're available in the Enum module. You wrote all these functions to understand how to create higher-order functions. From now on, you'll use them directly from the Enum module. Now we'll experiment with more useful higher-order functions from that module, starting with ones you've built. Open your IEx and try this:

```
iex> Enum.each(["dogs", "cats", "flowers"], &(IO.puts String.upcase(&1)))
DOGS
CATS
FLOWERS
iex> Enum.map(["dogs", "cats", "flowers"], &String.capitalize/1)
["Dogs", "Cats", "Flowers"]
iex> Enum.reduce([10, 5, 5, 10], 0, &+/2)
30
iex> Enum.filter(["a", "b", "c", "d"], &(&1 > "b"))
["c", "d"]
```

The Enum functions work like our homemade functions. The Enum module has many useful functions; it's easy to guess what they do from their names. Let's take a quick look:

```
iex> Enum.count(["dogs", "cats", "flowers"])
3
iex> Enum.uniq(["a", "a", "b", "b", "b", "c"])
["a", "b", "c"]
iex> Enum.sum([10, 5, 5, 10])
30
iex> Enum.sort(["c", "b", "d", "a"], &<=/2)
["a", "b", "c", "d"]
iex> Enum.sort(["c", "b", "d", "a"], &>=/2)
["d", "c", "b", "a"]
iex> Enum.member?([10, 20, 12], 10)
true
iex> Enum.join(["apples", "hot dogs", "flowers"], ", ")
"apples, hot dogs, flowers"
```

The count/1 function returns the total number of elements, and uniq/1 returns a new list without duplicated elements. sum/1 returns the sum of all numbers in a list, member?/2 checks if an item exists in a list, and join/2 combines the list items in one string. The sort/2 is a higher-order function that accepts a function comparing the elements in a list. The Enum functions work with any data type that respects the Enumerable *protocol*.[1] Take a look:

```
iex> upcase = fn {_key, value} -> String.upcase(value) end
iex> Enum.map(%{name: "willy", last_name: "wonka"}, upcase)
["WONKA", "WILLY"]
```

The map is a data type that implements the Enumerable protocol, so you can use it with the Enum module functions. On each iteration of a map structure, we have a tuple with two elements: one for the map key and the other for the value. We'll see more about protocols in Chapter 6, *Designing Your Elixir Applications*, on page 105.

In the Enum module, we also have useful and complex higher-order functions that take two functions in the argument. For example, Enum.group_by/3 receives a function that applies grouping criteria, and it takes a function that generates the values for each group. Let's try it with a list that contains medals and the players who earned them. Create the following medals variable:

```
iex> medals = [
  %{medal: :gold, player: "Anna"},
  %{medal: :silver, player: "Joe"},
  %{medal: :gold, player: "Zoe"},
  %{medal: :bronze, player: "Anna"},
  %{medal: :silver, player: "Anderson"},
  %{medal: :silver, player: "Peter"}
]
```

Now let's show the players that have won each type of medal. To do it, we need to group by medal type (gold, silver, or bronze), and for each group we need to build a list with players' names. Using recursive functions manually isn't easy, but using Enum.group_by/3 can be simple. Try it:

```
iex> Enum.group_by(medals, &(&1.medal), &(&1.player))
%{bronze: ["Anna"], gold: ["Anna", "Zoe"], silver: ["Joe", "Anderson", "Peter"]}
```

We've done a great operation in one line of code. The grouping-criteria function should return a value that will be used to group the items that have identical values. The anonymous function we passed &(&1.medal) returns the value of the medal; that can be :gold, :silver, or :bronze. Then the second function should return a value that goes in the list of each group. Next we use &(&1.player), which returns the player name. With this simple call, we've built a map that contains the players grouped by the medals they've won.

---

1.   https://hexdocs.pm/elixir/Enumerable.html

The flexible and reusable functions of the Enum module are very common in daily tasks, so take time to read about the Enum module and play with its functions. It will help you create simple code since you're taking advantage of the facilities Elixir provides.

## Using Comprehensions

Elixir has the for special form that offers a shortcut syntax over the most basic operations of enumerables—it is also known as a *comprehension*. We can iterate, map, and filter easily. Take a look:

```
iex> for a <- ["dogs", "cats", "flowers"], do: String.upcase(a)
["DOGS", "CATS", "FLOWERS"]
```

The expression after for is a generator expression that will assign each item of the list to the variable a. The result of the expression in the do option will be in the new list. We can have more than one generator:

```
iex> for a <- ["Willy", "Anna"], b <- ["Math", "English"], do: {a, b}
[{"Willy", "Math"}, {"Willy", "English"}, {"Anna", "Math"}, {"Anna", "English"}]
```

We've associated each student with a discipline using two generators. We can filter using pattern matching, and the items that don't match will be ignored:

```
iex> parseds = for i <- ["10", "hot dogs", "20" ], do: Integer.parse(i)
[{10, ""}, :error, {20, ""}]
iex> for {n, _} <- parseds, do: n
[10, 20]
```

We can also filter with an expression for truthy values:

```
iex> for n <- [1, 2, 3, 4, 5, 6, 7], n > 3, do: n
[4, 5, 6, 7]
```

n > 3 is a filter expression that will check if the number is greater than 3. The comprehensions are a nice syntax shortcut with a lot of use cases. You can learn more in the Elixir official documentation.[2]

## Pipelining Your Functions

Elixir has the famous *pipe* operator that's useful for combining functions to achieve a greater goal. It has a delightful syntax to execute many functions in sequence, and it's easy to read and understand. Other functional languages have a higher-order function that can *compose* functions. Elixir doesn't have a built-in function or an operator for function composition, but we can create it ourselves by using the *pipe* operator to combine two functions. Function

---

2. https://hexdocs.pm/elixir/Kernel.SpecialForms.html#for/1

composition and the pipe operator are useful for creating maintainable code by combining many small and focused routines. Let's see them in action, and you'll understand why you should prefer the pipe operator.

First, let's create a function that composes functions in a HighOrderFunctions module. Create this higher_order_functions.ex file:

```
higher_order_functions/higher_order_functions.ex
defmodule HigherOrderFunctions do
  def compose(f, g) do
    fn arg -> f.(g.(arg)) end
  end
end
```

The function compose/2 receives two functions, and builds a new one that accepts one argument. The function executes the g function with the given argument and calls f with the result. This function permits wrapping two function calls in one. We can use it like this:

```
iex> c("higher_order_functions.ex")
iex> import HighOrderFunctions
iex> first_letter_and_upcase = compose(&String.upcase/1, &String.first/1)
iex> first_letter_and_upcase.("works")
"W"
iex> first_letter_and_upcase.("combined")
"C"
```

We pass two functions to compose/2, and it combines them and creates one. Then we can use the returning function anytime we want. Since Elixir doesn't have a special syntax for function composition, combining more than two functions can be very confusing. The Elixir alternative is to use the *pipe* and *capture* operators. Let's build the same code again, combining those operators:

```
iex> first_letter_and_upcase = &(&1 |> String.first |> String.upcase)
iex> first_letter_and_upcase.("works")
"W"
iex> first_letter_and_upcase.("combined")
"C"
```

Different and beautiful, right? When we put a function call after the |>, Elixir takes the result evaluated in the previous expression and passes in the first argument of the function call. Let's try an explicit version of the code and see what's happening step by step:

```
iex> "works" |> String.first
"w"
iex> "w" |> String.upcase
"W"
```

```
iex> "works" |> String.first |> String.upcase
"W"
```

It takes the evaluated value of the expression before the |> and passes it to the
next function call as the first parameter. This syntax shines when we have to
combine more than two functions. Let's create a bigger function that will receive
some text and capitalize each word. For example, when it receives "a whole new
world," it returns "A Whole New World." Let's call this function capitalize_words and
put it in a module MyString. Let's write it only with simple functions:

higher_order_functions/my_string.ex
```
def capitalize_words(title) do
  words = String.split(title)
  capitalized_words = Enum.map(words, &String.capitalize/1)
  Enum.join(capitalized_words, " ")
end
```

Before we go into the implementation details, let's see it working in an IEx
session:

```
iex> c("my_string.ex")
iex> MyString.capitalize_words("a whole new world")
"A Whole New World"
```

The first step of the function is to split the text with whitespace to have a list
of words. Then we capitalize each word and join them all in a sentence, again
separating each word with whitespace. Note that for each step we put the
result in a variable to make clear each transformation we're doing. If we want
to get rid of the variables in the function, the basic way to combine functions
is to use them directly in the function call. You don't need to write the following
code; just take a look at how it can be done:

higher_order_functions/my_string.ex
```
def capitalize_words(title) do
  Enum.join(
    Enum.map(
      String.split(title),
      &String.capitalize/1
    ), " "
  )
end
```

We have a readability problem here: the first step of the data transformation
is in the middle of the functions, and to follow the order of execution you
must read backward. It's counterintuitive and hard to maintain. We can chain
the function calls to express a pipeline of data transformation using the pipe
operator. Let's rewrite our capitalize_words/1 in the Elixir way:

```
higher_order_functions/my_string.ex
def capitalize_words(title) do
  title
  |> String.split
  |> Enum.map(&String.capitalize/1)
  |> Enum.join(" ")
end
```

Look at the awesomeness of that code. Let's read it step by step: we start with the title variable, then we split and capitalize each word and join the words with whitespaces. The transformation of the title is expressed in a clean way. The order in which we read the code is the same order as the actual transformation. The pipe operator in Elixir is the best option to express a series of function calls. Now let's see what's happening in detail. Open your IEx and try the following expression:

```
iex> "a whole new world" |> String.split
["a", "whole", "new", "world"]
```

Elixir is taking the "a whole new world" string and passing it to String.split/1. For simple function calls, it's preferable to avoid the pipe syntax; the String.split("a whole new world"), for example, has better readability, and reads even better when you call a function with multiple arguments. Now let's add one more function call:

```
iex> "a whole new world" |> String.split |> Enum.map(&String.capitalize/1)
["A", "Whole", "New", "World"]
```

After splitting the string, the next function of the pipeline is Enum.map/2. That function takes two arguments, and the first will be provided from the previous expression. Then our work is to fill the second argument; we pass the function String.capitalize/1. Note that when the function has multiple arguments, it's important to call the function with parentheses; otherwise, Elixir can get lost in the pipeline of functions and an error will be raised. Using the pipe operator, the process of data transformation is clean and direct. We can also rewrite our capitalize_words/1 function to use helper functions:

```
higher_order_functions/my_string.ex
def capitalize_words(title) do
  title
  |> String.split
  |> capitalize_all
  |> join_with_whitespace
end

def capitalize_all(words) do
  Enum.map(words, &String.capitalize/1)
end
```

```
def join_with_whitespace(words) do
  Enum.join(words, " ")
end
```

We've created some auxiliary functions that give more meaning to code. We have capitalize_all/1, which receives a list of words and returns a list of capitalized words. And we've created join_with_whitespace/1, which receives a list of words and returns them joined with whitespace. It's good practice to create small functions with meaningful names. The function composition is a good concept, and Elixir has the pipe operator that is useful not only for composing functions but also for chaining many function calls in a way that makes the data-transformation steps clear, leading to code that is easier to write and understand.

# Be Lazy

Wait! I'm not telling you to put the book away and pass the entire day watching movies. I'm talking about *lazy evaluation* in programming. Lazy evaluation is when we write a series of instructions that won't be executed right now. Instead, they will wait for a trigger that will tell them the right moment to run. It's like if a friend of yours is cooking a roast turkey for Christmas and gives you an instruction to remove it from the oven. You can't take it out right when she tells you—that would be too soon. Instead, you need to wait for that little red thing in the turkey to pop up; that's the right moment.

Lazy operations provide alternative techniques of programming and creating efficient programs. In functional programming, higher-order functions are useful for working with lazy computation because we can pass functions that will be executed later, at an appropriate moment. We'll discuss some lazy evaluation techniques with higher-order functions, starting with delaying a function's execution.

## Delay the Function Call

Sometimes you want to give developers the flexibility to decide when a function will be evaluated, by building a new function using the existing one. Other functional languages have currying, which is a feature that delays a function's evaluation when you pass fewer arguments than the function requires. Elixir has *partial application*, a feature you can use to postpone a function's execution by wrapping it in a new function and fixing a value to any of the function's arguments.

While you can simulate function currying in Elixir (Patrik Storm covers how to do it in a fantastic article, "Function Currying in Elixir"[3]), it is not very

---

3.   http://blog.patrikstorm.com/function-currying-in-elixir

useful because the most important and the most often changed argument in Elixir's functions is always the first argument. Currying requires that you pass values to the arguments in sequence, making the last argument the most important because it will trigger the function call. Partial application doesn't care which argument is the most important, since you can pass a fixed value in any argument position you want—that's why it works better in Elixir. Let's try partial application by building an example.

Let's imagine we want to build a word by passing a list of positions that use a given series of letters to build words. This series of letters works like an alphabet. For example, if the function receives the series "aorxd" and a list [4, 1, 1, 2], it returns the string "door." Let's create a module WordBuilder and write the following code:

```
higher_order_functions/0/word_builder.ex
defmodule WordBuilder do
  def build(alphabet, positions) do
    letters = Enum.map(positions, String.at(alphabet))
    Enum.join(letters)
  end
end
```

We can try it using IEx:

```
iex> c("word_builder.ex")
iex> WordBuilder.build("world", [4, 1, 1, 2])
** (UndefinedFunctionError) undefined function: String.at/1
```

The code didn't work. We can't pass just one argument to String.at/2 because Elixir will try to evaluate it and String.at/1 doesn't exist. In Elixir, functions with different arities are different functions; they have a fixed number of arguments. If Elixir had support for curried functions, it would have returned a function that would expect the remaining arguments. Anonymous functions with closures allow us to do partial application. It permits us to set values to arguments of a function without invoking the function, giving us more flexibility to decide when it should be executed. For example, let's apply the partial application in our build function:

```
higher_order_functions/word_builder.ex
def build(alphabet, positions) do
  partial = fn at -> String.at(alphabet, at) end
  letters = Enum.map(positions, partial)
  Enum.join(letters)
end
```

We wrapped String.at/2 with an anonymous function that takes one argument. We took advantage of closures, referencing the alphabet variable, making our anonymous function remember its value. Then our anonymous function only needs the position to return the correct letter. Try it:

```
iex> c("word_builder.ex")
iex> WordBuilder.build("world", [4, 1, 1, 2])
"door"
```

It's common in Elixir for simple partial applications to use the function-capturing syntax. We can refactor our code to write something like this:

higher_order_functions/word_builder.ex
```
def build(alphabet, positions) do
  letters = Enum.map(positions, &(String.at(alphabet, &1)))
  Enum.join(letters)
end
```

You can try it again in your IEx; it will have the same effect. The partial application permits you to delay a function call, predetermining some values in the function call arguments and using values from closures. It gives you more flexibility to build functions, helping you solve problems where some arguments of a function call must be a fixed value.

## Working with the Infinite

The infinite can have a lot of definitions in cosmology, philosophy, theology, or mathematics. For programming, we can think of it as something that is *always expanding*; there's no limit. Examples include a web server that is always handling new connections, a messaging broker handling upcoming events, and a game console that listens to the players' controller inputs. In Elixir, we have the *streams* type that represents a flow of data that may not have an end. Together with this data type, we have the Stream module that contains many higher-order functions to operate and create our streams. Let's explore how to work with an endless stream of data.

The simplest stream we can create in Elixir uses the range literal. Try it in your IEx:

```
iex> range = 1..10
1..10
```

range is a lazy collection. Lazy collections are evaluated only when necessary. The range value only has the instructions to count from one to ten; it doesn't put all the numbers in memory. range values from one to ten and from one to ten billion take the same space in memory. If we want to see all the numbers, we need to do some operation that accesses all of them. For example, we can navigate through each item using Enum.each/2:

```
iex> Enum.each(range, &IO.puts/1)
1
2
# ...
10
:ok
```

When we use the each/2 function, we tell Elixir it's time to evaluate each number of that collection, one at a time. Let's try an advanced example. In Chapter 4, *Diving into Recursion*, on page 59, we built a factorial example using recursive functions. Now let's use a different implementation of the factorial algorithm using streams. Let's start with a range that will work with numbers from one to ten million. Let's build the Factorial module:

```
higher_order_functions/finite/factorial.ex
defmodule Factorial do
  def of(0), do: 1
  def of(n) when n > 0 do
    1..10_000_000
      |> Enum.take(n)
      |> Enum.reduce(&(&1* &2))
  end
end
```

You can try it using IEx:

```
iex> c("factorial.ex")
iex> Factorial.of(5)
120
```

It's a different way of thinking about how to solve the factorial problem. We didn't use recursive functions that multiply and decrement the number. Instead, we solved the problem with a collection. We can think of the integers as a collection. We take n numbers from it, and we multiply each of them with the accumulator, from smallest to largest. It's very fast! We used a stream because it's lazy, so the ten million numbers are not evaluated right away.

Everything is working, and it's great. But it has a limitation; it only works up to ten million. That's a huge number that will solve most use cases, but we can do better. It should work using all the machine resources, without boundaries, to the infinite. Infinity is always expanding. In Elixir, we can represent a collection that is always expanding using the higher-order function Stream.iterate/2.

It creates a stream where the items are evaluated dynamically. Every time something asks for an item, the dynamic stream will determine the next element. That function expects a starting value and an increment function. The increment function receives the previous value, and it's our job to say how to calculate the next value. Let's see it in action; try this in your IEx:

```
iex> integers = Stream.iterate(1, fn previous -> previous + 1 end)
iex> Enum.take(integers, 5)
[1, 2, 3, 4, 5]
```

We created a stream with an endless data flow of numbers that increment by one with each iteration. We just took the first five numbers, but we can make it run forever. If you want to see it counting forever, run the following code and be prepared to halt the process:

```
iex> Enum.each(integers, &IO.puts/1)
1
2
3
#...
```

Now let's improve our factorial function to use infinite numbers:

higher_order_functions/infinite/factorial.ex
```
defmodule Factorial do
  def of(0), do: 1
  def of(n) when n > 0 do
    Stream.iterate(1, &(&1 + 1))
      |> Enum.take(n)
      |> Enum.reduce(&(&1* &2))
  end
end
```

Try it in your IEx; it will work with any number:

```
iex> c("factorial.ex")
iex> Factorial.of(5)
120
iex> Factorial.of(10)
3628800
```

Elixir has other useful functions to generate infinite collections, such as Stream.cycle/1. With the cycle function, we can easily create an infinite collection that loops through the same items. Let's say it's Halloween and we need to give candy to kids who come to our house. We have chocolates, jellies, and mints, and we want to distribute each candy type equally. In other words, one kid will receive chocolate, another jelly, another mint, another chocolate, and the cycle repeats. Let's build this example in Elixir by creating the Halloween module:

higher_order_functions/halloween.ex

```
defmodule Halloween do
  def give_candy(kids) do
    ~w(chocolate jelly mint)
    |> Stream.cycle
    |> Enum.zip(kids)
  end
end
```

Before going into implementation details, let's test our code in IEx:

```
iex> c("halloween.ex")
iex> Halloween.give_candy(~w(Mike Anna Ted Mary Alex Emma))
[{"chocolate", "Mike"}, {"jelly", "Anna"}, {"mint", "Ted"},
 {"chocolate", "Mary"}, {"jelly", "Alex"}, {"mint", "Emma"}]
```

The return of the function is a list of tuples, where each tuple has a kid and their candy. Thanks to the Stream.cycle/1 function, after we give a mint we return to the beginning of the list and start to give chocolate again.

The ~w is the sigil for word lists. The Enum.zip/2 function creates a new list by combining two lists where the elements of the new list will follow the same order as the original lists. Each new element is a tuple with one item of each list. One list is endless and cycles between chocolate, jelly, and mint, and the other list is finite and has the kids' names. When we zip them together, the function will stop combining them when it reaches the end of the shorter list. We also have the Stream.zip/2 to use if we want to create a lazy combination.

The lazy computation permits us to represent the infinite collection and gives us new possibilities to create different solutions. The Elixir Stream modules provide useful higher-order functions that help developers work with lazy collections easily.

## Pipelining Data Streams

In this section, you'll learn how to combine Elixir pipe operator and streams, creating a pipeline of tasks to consume a data stream. We can do it in two ways: eager or lazy. With the eager strategy, each computation will process all the items before sending them to the next computation. With the lazy approach, each computation can process a small number of elements and send them to the next computation. The effect is that the eager strategy will output a result only after all the items have been processed. The lazy strategy will start to produce a result after a small number of elements have been processed. Until now we have used a lot of the eager approach, and it has worked very well. In this section, we'll explore the benefits of the lazy strategy using lazy collections and Stream higher-order functions.

To better understand how eager and lazy evaluation work, think of a mechanized assembly line: it has a tray we can put items on, the assembly line will start to run, and the items will be processed sequentially by the machines that are connected to the tray. In the eager approach, all the elements on the tray must be processed by a machine before it lets them go on to the next step. So, if we have three items on the tray at the beginning, all of them must be processed by the machine and then sent onward. If someone is waiting for the result at the end of the assembly line, they will need to wait a long time to see something done. With lazy evaluation, each machine can process a small number of items and pass them onward rather than processing everything at once. So, if we have three items on the tray at the beginning, as soon as an item is processed by the first machine, it will be sent to the next machine without waiting for the other two items to finish. If someone is waiting for the result at the end of the assembly line, they will have fast feedback because the first item will reach the end of the line quickly.

Let's simulate this by building a ScrewsFactory module. It will be a simple version of the process of manufacturing screws. Our module will have a function that will receive several pieces of metal, and then it will apply a screw thread and head. Each step of our process will wait some number of milliseconds to simulate a process that takes time to finish. This forced wait time will be useful so we can better see the consequences of working with a huge quantity of screws. Write the module in a screws_factory.ex file:

```
higher_order_functions/0/screws_factory.ex
defmodule ScrewsFactory do
  def run(pieces) do
    pieces
    |> Enum.map(&add_thread/1)
    |> Enum.map(&add_head/1)
    |> Enum.each(&output/1)
  end

  defp add_thread(piece) do
    Process.sleep(50)
    piece <> "--"
  end

  defp add_head(piece) do
    Process.sleep(100)
    "o" <> piece
  end

  defp output(screw) do
    IO.inspect(screw)
  end
end
```

Before we discuss the details of the code, you can try it using IEx. Be ready to halt the program execution if you don't want to wait for it to finish:

```
iex> c("screws_factory.ex")
iex> metal_pieces = Enum.take(Stream.cycle(["-"]), 1000)
iex> ScrewsFactory.run(metal_pieces)
```

It's very slow to start manufacturing the screws because the approach we've taken here is the eager strategy. It first adds the screw thread to all the metal pieces. Then it adds the screw head to all the pieces. Finally, it starts to show the screws in the end of pipeline. That slow feedback is a common problem when we're trying to do a task for each item of a collection that takes some time—for example, accessing an external resource like a database or an API REST call. Each access takes a few milliseconds and degrades the performance. When we're working with just a few items we can't perceive the speed problem, but when we're working with hundreds of items the slowness will scream in our ears.

Eager computation can solve most of the problems if we don't need instant feedback. However, our screw factory will be more efficient if we have some screws ready to be packed before *all* the metal pieces are manufactured.

Let's change our implementation to a lazy strategy with Elixir streams:

```
higher_order_functions/screws_factory.ex
def run(pieces) do
  pieces
  |> Stream.map(&add_thread/1)
  |> Stream.map(&add_head/1)
  |> Enum.each(&output/1)
end
```

Let's process the file again:

```
iex> c("screws_factory.ex")
iex> ScrewsFactory.run(metal_pieces)
```

Now we have fast feedback of each item being processed! The amazing thing is that we didn't need to change our internal functions—only the pipeline. We use the Stream.map/1 in the beginning of the pipeline to create a stream. The next step of the pipeline adds another transformation on the stream. In the last step, we use Enum.each/2 to start to show the screws in the console by applying all defined transformations, one screw at a time.

The screw factory delivers the screws as soon as they're done. Let's imagine that our company executives are jubilant about the improvement, and they buy us new machines. The threading machine now can process 50 pieces at once, while the heading machine can process 100 pieces. With these new machines, we can be even more productive.

Let's change our code to add the new machines:

higher_order_functions/screws_factory.ex

```elixir
def run(pieces) do
  pieces
  |> Stream.chunk(50)
  |> Stream.flat_map(&add_thread/1)
  |> Stream.chunk(100)
  |> Stream.flat_map(&add_head/1)
  |> Enum.each(&output/1)
end

defp add_thread(pieces) do
  Process.sleep(50)
  Enum.map(pieces, &(&1 <> "--"))
end

defp add_head(pieces) do
  Process.sleep(100)
  Enum.map(pieces, &("o" <> &1))
end

defp output(screw) do
  IO.inspect(screw)
end
```

Now try it and see how fast it will process:

```elixir
iex> c("screws_factory.ex")
iex> ScrewsFactory.run(metal_pieces)
```

Super fast! Let's understand how we've done it, focusing first on the run/1 function. The new things here are Stream.chunk/2 and Stream.flat_map/2. The chunk function is responsible for accumulating some items before sending them to the next function. It creates a queue in our processing pipeline. When the queue is full or the stream is over, it sends the accumulated items to the next function in the pipeline. It can be easier to understand in isolation:

```elixir
iex> Enum.chunk([1, 2, 3, 4, 5, 6], 2)
[[1, 2], [3, 4], [5, 6]]
```

We're using Enum, but the Stream version operates in the same way. We've created a list of small lists that contain two accumulated items. Then comes the flat_map, which returns a new list, appending the enumerable result of the given function.

Let's see it working in isolation:

```
iex> Enum.flat_map([[1, 2], [3, 4], [5, 6]], &(&1))
[1, 2, 3, 4, 5, 6]
```

Then, having our flow of items in the flat form, we can accumulate again to create new groups of items for the next functions. Processing a bunch of elements simultaneously, in batches, has increased the overall speed. The speed benefit happened because the cost of processing one item or a bunch of items costs almost the same time.

The Stream higher-order functions and the lazy technique can help you create a program that works more efficiently by providing faster feedback. This is very useful when you have a pipeline with tasks that can take some time and you don't want to leave the consumer at the end of the pipeline waiting.

# Wrapping Up

You've seen the full power of functions. Higher-order functions play an important role in a lot of Elixir's core functions and libraries. Let's review what you've learned about higher-order functions in this chapter:

- They are very handy for creating useful functions with a simple interface.

- They are present everywhere, such as when working with lists, files, processes, and I/O.

- Elixir features such as the pipe operator and partial application are useful for combining functions and delaying function evaluation.

- They build a fundamental interface to functions that have lazy computation.

In the next chapter, we'll cover exciting features for designing our application entities. We'll see how to create structs, polymorphisms, and behaviours.

## Your Turn

- In Chapter 4, *Diving into Recursion*, on page 59, we built a module called EnchanterShop that transforms mundane items into magical items for sale. Build this module again, but now apply the higher-order functions that you learned in this chapter.

- In this chapter, we created a screw factory that processes metal pieces and generates screws. A new requirement has arrived for us: we now need to pack them. We can pack 30 screws per package, and it takes 70ms. A screw is packed when the resulting string is "|o---|". Change the ScrewsFactory module, adding the simulation of packing screws.

- Create a function that generates the Fibonacci sequence up to a given quantity.[4] Use streams to produce it. You'll need to take a look at the Stream.unfold/2 function. Tip: Try to make the recursive version first.

- Implement the Quicksort algorithm.[5] Tip: You can use the first item of the list to be the pivot, and employ the Enum.split_with/2 higher-order function.

4.   https://en.wikipedia.org/wiki/Fibonacci_number
5.   https://en.wikipedia.org/wiki/Quicksort

# CHAPTER 6

# Designing Your Elixir Applications

Software that solves real-world problems has to maintain and organize various files. It's important that you learn language features that will help you organize your code and design your application domain. A well-organized codebase makes it easier to fix bugs and add or change features. In this chapter, we'll build a game and you'll learn new techniques to build and design your own application. You'll learn how to design the application entities with Elixir structs. You'll see how to create polymorphic functions using Elixir *protocols*. You'll create function contracts with Elixir *behaviours*. The first step is to learn the basics of *Mix*, the essential tool to start any new Elixir project.

We'll use a lot of the concepts that we've already explored. For example, you'll see higher-order, recursive, and anonymous functions applied together to solve a problem. Be ready; you'll see and write a lot of code in this chapter. We'll move faster than in the previous chapters, focusing only on the new things.

## Starting Your Project with Mix

Mix is a command-line interface (CLI) tool that provides the essentials for building any Elixir application. Mix helps you create and maintain Elixir projects, providing tasks to compile, debug, test, and manage dependencies and your environment. All Elixir libraries and applications were built with Mix. It comes by default with Elixir; you don't need to install anything new. We'll use Mix CLI tasks to create the initial setup of the game, and the Mix module guidelines to build a command-line task to run the game. These are the essential features to build our small project. You can find other useful features in the Mix official documentation.[1] We'll begin by making sure we understand the application we'll build. Then we'll create the application's initial files and a command-line task to start the game.

---

1. https://hexdocs.pm/mix/Mix.html

## What We'll Build

We'll implement a small terminal game where the player must survive a dungeon full of monsters and traps. The player wakes up in a room and must walk through other rooms. The game ends when the player finds the exit. In each chamber, the player must decide what to do. The result of these decisions can lead the player to treasure, traps, enemies, more rooms to explore, or the exit. The game starts with the player choosing a hero to play as. The following diagram shows the game flow we'll build.

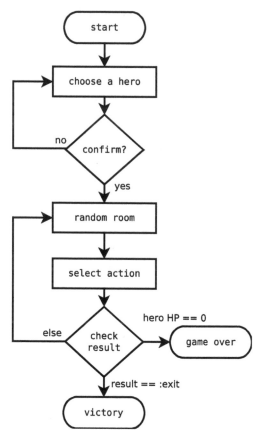

The hero has hit points, which are reduced by taking damage from fighting enemies or falling into traps. When the character reaches zero hit points, the player loses the game. The character's hit points can be restored by finding healing potions or resting in safe rooms. The challenge is to find the exit room before the hero reaches zero hit points. Now that you have the main idea of the game, let's start coding it.

## Running the new Task

The mix new task creates the initial structure to code your application. You just need to pass the application name, and it will do the rest. Let's run it to create the dungeon_crawl application:

```
$ mix new dungeon_crawl
* creating README.md
* creating .gitignore
* creating mix.exs
* creating config
* creating config/config.exs
* creating lib
* creating lib/dungeon_crawl.ex
* creating test
* creating test/test_helper.exs
* creating test/dungeon_crawl_test.exs

Your Mix project was created successfully.
You can use "mix" to compile it, test it, and more:

    cd dungeon_crawl
    mix test

Run "mix help" for more commands.
```

The output shows you the base structure of directories to start building your Elixir application. The most relevant directories for now are lib and test. The lib directory is where you'll put your application code. The test directory is where you'll put the code that checks the lib application code's correctness. The command output also shows you the next steps: cd dungeon_crawl to enter the application directory, and mix test to run the application tests. Let's do it:

```
$ cd dungeon_crawl
$ mix test
Compiling 1 file (.ex)
Generated dungeon_crawl app
..

Finished in 0.05 seconds
2 tests, 0 failures

Randomized with seed 841143
```

When we run the mix test task, it automatically detects the files that need to be compiled. Then it compiles the files and starts the application test suite. The output says we have two tests and they are passing. The tests run in random order, and we can repeat that order using the seed number. The first test is in test/dungeon_crawl_test.exs:

```
design_your_application/dungeon_crawl/test/dungeon_crawl_test.exs
defmodule DungeonCrawlTest do
  use ExUnit.Case
  doctest DungeonCrawl

  test "greets the world" do
    assert DungeonCrawl.hello() == :world
  end
end
```

In this file, we have new directives. use permits another module to take actions and inject code on the calling module. It adds new capabilities to the current module, mostly by using metaprogramming features. For example, when we add the directive use ExUnit.Case, we're adding the capacity to run tests and utility functions for testing to our DungeonCrawlTest module.

The directive doctest came from ExUnit.Case. It parses our module documentation, runs the code inside of it, and checks if it's working. Finally, we have the test code, which does a mere assertion: assert DungeonCrawl.hello() == :world. But wait. The mix test command output says that we have two tests; the second test is in lib/dungeon_crawl.ex file:

```
design_your_application/dungeon_crawl/lib/dungeon_crawl.ex
defmodule DungeonCrawl do
  @moduledoc """
  Documentation for DungeonCrawl.
  """

  @doc """
  Hello, world.

  ## Examples

      iex> DungeonCrawl.hello
      :world

  """
  def hello do
    :world
  end
end
```

In that file, we have a large documentation section. Thanks to the doctest directive, the second test that Elixir runs is to take the example of the documentation and see if that code works as expected. It's a very powerful feature to keep the documentation up to date, and it's a very useful feature for library maintainers. Testing and documentation are big subjects that this book doesn't cover. You can remove the test file, but if you want to learn more about it, take a look at the ExUnit official documentation.[2]

## Create the Start Task

Mix tasks are commands that you can invoke in the terminal that use Mix utilities—for example, commands like mix new and mix test are Mix tasks. We can add new tasks to our project by creating modules that follow the Mix.Task contract. These tasks help developers set up and automate procedures and provide a useful shortcut to run them. Let's build a task that starts our game. With it, we can see the game updates after changing the code. We can create a Mix task by building a module in the Mix.Tasks namespace, adding the use Mix.Task directive and implementing the run/1 function. The first step is to add the task file, following this directory structure:

```
lib
└── mix
    └── tasks
        └── start.ex
```

You can add a new Mix task by creating a new file in the directory lib/mix/tasks. We created start.ex. Now put this code inside:

design_your_application/tutorial/0/dungeon_crawl/lib/mix/tasks/start.ex
```
defmodule Mix.Tasks.Start do
  use Mix.Task

  def run(_), do: IO.puts "Hello, World!"
end
```

In this file, we're turning the module into a Mix task by using the use Mix.Task directive. We needed to put the name of our module in the namespace Mix.Tasks and create a run function that must accept one argument. That argument will be the parameters the user can pass when running a command. We're ignoring it because we only want to print a "Hello, World" message. Then we can execute the mix start task and see the resulting output:

```
$ mix start
Compiling 1 file (.ex)
Hello, World!
```

This is how you can create tasks to run any code you want in your application. The directory structure following the module namespaces isn't required. However, it's a good convention that this book and many applications follow. It keeps your code organized and makes your modules easier to find. You can

---

2. https://hexdocs.pm/ex_unit/ExUnit.html

see more options for creating Mix tasks by reading the Mix.Task module official documentation.[3]

# Designing Entities with Structs

Programming language entities and data types are not enough when you're building a larger application. We need to create new data entities to express the application domain. In Elixir, we employ structs. We covered how to *use* them in *Matching Structs*, on page 44, but now we'll see how to *create* them. We'll create a struct that represents the player's hero. Then we'll organize our application, separating the domain entities from CLI code by listing the heroes' options to the player. Then we'll use some Mix command-line functions to let the player choose a hero. The first step is to build a struct to describe the Character domain entity.

## Creating the Character with Structs

We'll build a struct that will hold all the character's related properties. The character will be consistent across the entire application since structs don't let us add new attributes beyond their definition. Let's create a file that will have the struct in the following directory, under lib:

```
lib
├── dungeon_crawl
│   ├── character.ex
└── mix
```

When building Elixir's applications it's a good practice to put all the modules and related code under your application domain namespace. The Character struct will be under the DungeonCrawl game namespace, then inside of the dungeon_crawl folder. In the file character.ex, let's define the character struct:

design_your_application/tutorial/0/dungeon_crawl/lib/dungeon_crawl/character.ex
```
defmodule DungeonCrawl.Character do
  defstruct name: nil,
            description: nil,
            hit_points: 0,
            max_hit_points: 0,
            attack_description: nil,
            damage_range: nil
end
```

The module Character lives inside the DungeonCrawl namespace. We used the defstruct directive to create the character struct, passing a keyword list. The

---

key is the attribute name, and the value will be the default value when we initialize a struct. Let's see the purpose of each attribute:

- name—a name that differentiates one character from others

- description—a long description that explains the character's advantages and disadvantages

- hit_points—current hit points

- max_hit_points—the maximum hit points a character can have

- attack_description—the text that explains how a character attacks another

- damage_range—the minimum and maximum damage a character can cause when attacking

Let's try our struct initialization inside an IEx shell. We can run a Mix task to start the shell and load all modules automatically. Run the following command in the dungeon_crawl folder:

```
$ iex -S mix
Compiling 1 file (.ex)
Generated dungeon_crawl app
Interactive Elixir
```

The -S flag tells IEx to run a script on launch; passing mix will run the project's mix task, compiling and loading the project's modules. We can create characters using our struct with the IEx session loaded:

```
iex> warrior = %DungeonCrawl.Character{name: "Warrior"}
%DungeonCrawl.Character{attack_description: nil, damage_range: nil,
 description: nil, hit_points: 0, max_hit_points: 0, name: "Warrior"}
iex> warrior.name
"Warrior"
```

We've covered how to create a struct, define attributes, and initialize structs. Structs permit us to define a group of related attributes that represent a domain entity in our application.

## Listing the Heroes

The next step is to make the game display a list of heroes to the player. The actions of displaying an interface and displaying the heroes list are two different contexts. You'll learn how to separate them. First, let's create the heroes list by creating the heroes.ex file in the lib/dungeon_crawl folder. Your directory structure should look like this:

```
lib/
└── dungeon_crawl
    ├── character.ex
    └── heroes.ex
```

In heroes.ex, build the following module:

design_your_application/dungeon_crawl/lib/dungeon_crawl/heroes.ex
```elixir
defmodule DungeonCrawl.Heroes do
  alias DungeonCrawl.Character

  def all, do: [
    %Character{
      name: "Knight",
      description: "Knight has strong defense and consistent damage.",
      hit_points: 18,
      max_hit_points: 18,
      damage_range: 4..5,
      attack_description: "a sword"
    },
    %Character{
      name: "Wizard",
      description: "Wizard has strong attack, but low health.",
      hit_points: 8,
      max_hit_points: 8,
      damage_range: 6..10,
      attack_description: "a fireball"
    },
    %Character{
      name: "Rogue",
      description: "Rogue has high variability of attack damage.",
      hit_points: 12,
      max_hit_points: 12,
      damage_range: 1..12,
      attack_description: "a dagger"
    },
  ]
end
```

We've made a list of heroes using the DungeonCrawl.Character struct. The first line of our module uses the alias directive. This alias creates a shortcut, allowing us to type only %Character to reference the struct. The heroes described here are just suggestions; you can build your heroes with your rules. Have fun!

To display the heroes, we need to build a central point of interaction with the player. We'll create a folder to store the CLI code and a main.ex file that will start and end our game. Create the following file and directory structure:

```
lib
├── dungeon_crawl
│   └── cli
│       └── main.ex
│
```

For now, main.ex will contain a welcome message with the introduction of the game:

design_your_application/tutorial/0/dungeon_crawl/lib/dungeon_crawl/cli/main.ex
```
defmodule DungeonCrawl.CLI.Main do
  alias Mix.Shell.IO, as: Shell

  def start_game do
    welcome_message()
  end

  defp welcome_message do
    Shell.info("== Dungeon Crawl ===")
    Shell.info("You awake in a dungeon full of monsters.")
    Shell.info("You need to survive and find the exit.")
  end
end
```

DungeonCrawl.CLI.Main will orchestrate the game. Let's see some details of the implementation. Mix.Shell.IO brings useful functions to interact with the terminal. For example, it has the yes?/1 function to get a positive or negative answer from the player. We used info to print messages with the alias Shell to avoid typing the full qualified name of Mix.Shell.IO. Now we need to invoke the start_game/0 function from the Mix task that we created in the previous section:

design_your_application/dungeon_crawl/lib/mix/tasks/start.ex
```
defmodule Mix.Tasks.Start do
  use Mix.Task

  def run(_), do: DungeonCrawl.CLI.Main.start_game
end
```

Then we can run the game with mix start and see the introduction.

```
$ mix start
== Dungeon Crawl ===
You awake in a dungeon full of monsters.
You need to survive and find the exit.
```

Now, it's time to list all available heroes for the player. Let's build this functionality in a separate module called DungeonCrawl.CLI.HeroChoice that will be in lib/dungeon_crawl/cli/hero_choice.ex. Create the following code:

design_your_application/tutorial/0/dungeon_crawl/lib/dungeon_crawl/cli/hero_choice.ex
```elixir
defmodule DungeonCrawl.CLI.HeroChoice do
  alias Mix.Shell.IO, as: Shell

  def start do
    Shell.cmd("clear")
    Shell.info("Start by choosing your hero:")

    heroes = DungeonCrawl.Heroes.all()

    heroes
    |> Enum.map(&(&1.name))
    |> display_options
  end

  def display_options(options) do
    options
    |> Enum.with_index(1)
    |> Enum.each(fn {option, index} ->
      Shell.info("#{index} - #{option}")
    end)

    options
  end
end
```

We are again using the Mix.Shell.IO utilities to work with the shell. This time we're using cmd/1. It allows us to send terminal commands to our current shell. We clear the screen before showing the user the available heroes. Then we take the list of heroes, map their names, and display them in a numbered list, starting with 1. We used the Enum.with_index function to generate a list of tuples that contain the heroes' names and their corresponding index numbers. Now let's invoke this module in our DungeonCrawl.CLI.Main function:

design_your_application/tutorial/1/dungeon_crawl/lib/dungeon_crawl/cli/main.ex
```elixir
defmodule DungeonCrawl.CLI.Main do
  alias Mix.Shell.IO, as: Shell

  def start_game do
    welcome_message()
    Shell.prompt("Press Enter to continue")
    hero_choice()
  end

  defp welcome_message do
    Shell.info("== Dungeon Crawl ===")
    Shell.info("You awake in a dungeon full of monsters.")
    Shell.info("You need to survive and find the exit.")
  end

  defp hero_choice do
    DungeonCrawl.CLI.HeroChoice.start()
  end
end
```

Now we can run it with mix start and see what we've done.

```
Start by choosing your hero:
1 - Knight
2 - Wizard
3 - Rogue
```

We've separated functions of CLI interactions in a different namespace to create a boundary. (Creating boundaries makes your code consistent and easier to maintain.) The next step is to ask the player to choose a hero.

## Choosing a Hero

After the game lists the heroes, the player must type a number to choose one. Let's build that functionality. First, we need to generate a question with the numbers that player can choose, get the player input, parse it, and select the corresponding hero. Improve your lib/dungeon_crawl/cli/hero_choice.ex with the following code:

design_your_application/tutorial/1/dungeon_crawl/lib/dungeon_crawl/cli/hero_choice.ex
```
def start do
  Shell.cmd("clear")
  Shell.info("Start by choosing your hero:")

  heroes = DungeonCrawl.Heroes.all()
  find_hero_by_index = &Enum.at(heroes, &1)

  heroes
  |> Enum.map(&(&1.name))
  |> display_options
  |> generate_question
  |> Shell.prompt
  |> parse_answer
  |> find_hero_by_index.()
  |> confirm_hero
end
```

The pipeline of functions says to take the heroes' names, display them, generate a question, ask the user for input, parse the user's answer, find the corresponding hero, and confirm the player choice. The pipeline starts with a list of heroes and ends with the chosen hero. So, after listing the heroes, we must implement the generate_question/1 function:

design_your_application/tutorial/1/dungeon_crawl/lib/dungeon_crawl/cli/hero_choice.ex
```
defp generate_question(options) do
  options = Enum.join(1..Enum.count(options),",")
  "Which one? [#{options}]\n"
end
```

It starts generating a string by building a range from 1 to the number of elements and joins them with a comma, generating something like "1,2,3". It joins the question and the numbers and returns the result. The next step of the pipeline uses this result, invoking the prompt/1 function. It works like this: it accepts a question in the argument, displays the question, awaits an input, and returns what the user has typed. With the user input, we need to parse it. We can do it with parse_answer/1:

design_your_application/tutorial/1/dungeon_crawl/lib/dungeon_crawl/cli/hero_choice.ex
```
defp parse_answer(answer) do
  {option, _} = Integer.parse(answer)
  option - 1
end
```

It tries to parse an integer from the user input, then subtracts one to get the index of the hero. You don't need to worry now what happens if a user types a number that doesn't exist, or something like *hot dogs*. We'll handle unexpected events in Chapter 7, *Handling Impure Functions*, on page 139. You can keep coding for now and assume that nothing bad will happen.

The program uses the find_hero_by_index/1 anonymous function defined at start/0 to receive the parsed answer and return the hero. That anonymous function is necessary because we can't use Enum.at/2 directly in the pipeline. The Enum.at/2 argument is a list, and we need to pass the hero index. The anonymous function also references the heroes variable by taking advantage of closures. The last step is to confirm the player option with the chosen hero:

design_your_application/tutorial/1/dungeon_crawl/lib/dungeon_crawl/cli/hero_choice.ex
```
defp confirm_hero(chosen_hero) do
  Shell.cmd("clear")
  Shell.info(chosen_hero.description)
  if Shell.yes?("Confirm?"), do: chosen_hero, else: start()
end
```

In the confirm_hero/1 function we clear the screen, display the details of the chosen hero, and ask the user to confirm the choice. Windows users need to replace the clear command with cls to clear the screen. We use the yes?/1 function from Mix.Shell.IO to get the user input, check if it's a positive answer, and parse it to a Boolean value. For example, when the user answers *y*, it parses to true and we return the chosen hero. If the user answers *n*, we restart the process by making a recursive call to the start/0 function. Let's run mix start to try what we've built:

```
Start by choosing your hero:
1 - Knight
2 - Wizard
3 - Rogue
Which one? [1,2,3]
```

⇒ **1**
‹

```
Knight has strong defense and consistent damage.
Confirm? [Yn]
```
⇒ **yes**

We've made the first part of the game. You've learned how to create structs, separate different code contexts in different namespaces, and interact with the user via the command-line interface. In the next section, we'll add more features, increasing our codebase. A kid needs good habits to have healthy growth, and it's the same thing for your codebase. As you develop new features, you'll learn refactoring techniques and how to use Elixir's *protocols*, good habits to make your codebase have healthy growth.

# Using Protocols to Create Polymorphic Functions

Elixir's *protocol* is a feature that lets you create a single interface that various data types can implement. Using that, you can have *polymorphism*: a single interface that works with different data types. If you came from object-oriented languages like Java, you'll see that it's very similar to how interfaces work. Elixir protocols will help you create simple interfaces, leading to a better codebase design.

In this section we'll explore more about structs, including structs that reference other structs. We'll refactor our code to create a reusable module that shares functions between heroes and action selections. Then we'll build polymorphic functions with *protocols* to display heroes and actions. The first step is to define the essential attributes of the rooms and their actions.

## Building Structs That Use Structs

When the hero is in a room, the player can choose an action and face the consequences. We have two new structs to build and one will reference the other. The Room struct will have many Action structs. Let's define the room action module in lib/dungeon_crawl/room/action.ex. Then we'll add the following module to the file:

design_your_application/tutorial/0/dungeon_crawl/lib/dungeon_crawl/room/action.ex
```
defmodule DungeonCrawl.Room.Action do
  alias DungeonCrawl.Room.Action
  defstruct label: nil, id: nil

  def forward, do: %Action{id: :forward, label: "Move forward."}
  def rest, do: %Action{id: :rest, label: "Take a better look and rest."}
  def search, do: %Action{id: :search, label: "Search the room."}
end
```

The DungeonCrawl.Room.Action struct has id and label attributes. We also created helper functions to build common actions that we'll need to build the rooms. The next step is to create the room module. Create lib/dungeon_crawl/room.ex and add this code to it:

```
design_your_application/tutorial/0/dungeon_crawl/lib/dungeon_crawl/room.ex
defmodule DungeonCrawl.Room do
  alias DungeonCrawl.Room

  import DungeonCrawl.Room.Action

  defstruct description: nil, actions: []

  def all, do: [
    %Room{
      description: "You found a quiet place. Looks safe for a little nap.",
      actions: [forward(), rest()],
    },
  ]
end
```

The DungeonCrawl.Room struct has description and actions attributes. The module has the function all/0 that lists all available rooms. We've defined a struct that contains other structs to describe the room and its actions. For now we're making only one room to create the room actions listing and selection. Later we'll come back here and add more rooms.

## Refactoring Modules and Reusing Functions

Now we'll implement the interaction for the player to choose a room action when the hero is in the room. The process is very similar to what we did for hero choice. It means that we can reuse a lot of functions. But first we need to refactor our code. *Refactoring* is organizing the code to better accommodate new features without breaking the existing ones. It avoids duplicated code and promotes better abstractions. Let's create a reusable module that will allow for hero and action listing and choice. Let's create a module in lib/dungeon_crawl/cli/base_commands.ex and put all the reusable functions from hero_choice.ex in it:

```
design_your_application/tutorial/0/dungeon_crawl/lib/dungeon_crawl/cli/base_commands.ex
defmodule DungeonCrawl.CLI.BaseCommands do
  alias Mix.Shell.IO, as: Shell

  def display_options(options) do
    options
    |> Enum.with_index(1)
    |> Enum.each(fn {option, index} ->
      Shell.info("#{index} - #{option}")
    end)
```

```
    options
  end

  def generate_question(options) do
    options = Enum.join(1..Enum.count(options),",")
    "Which one? [#{options}]\n"
  end

  def parse_answer(answer) do
    {option, _} = Integer.parse(answer)
    option - 1
  end
end
```

Note that we're moving the reusable functions and making them public by replacing defp with def. We can now make the HeroChoice module reuse these functions by importing the BaseCommands module. Your module should look like this:

design_your_application/tutorial/2/dungeon_crawl/lib/dungeon_crawl/cli/hero_choice.ex

```
defmodule DungeonCrawl.CLI.HeroChoice do
  alias Mix.Shell.IO, as: Shell
  import DungeonCrawl.CLI.BaseCommands

  def start do
    Shell.cmd("clear")
    Shell.info("Start by choosing your hero:")

    heroes = DungeonCrawl.Heroes.all()
    find_hero_by_index = &Enum.at(heroes, &1)

    heroes
    |> Enum.map(&(&1.name))
    |> display_options
    |> generate_question
    |> Shell.prompt
    |> parse_answer
    |> find_hero_by_index.()
    |> confirm_hero
  end

  defp confirm_hero(chosen_hero) do
    Shell.cmd("clear")
    Shell.info(chosen_hero.description)
    if Shell.yes?("Confirm?"), do: chosen_hero, else: start()
  end
end
```

Then we can finally write the module that will handle the interaction to choose the room actions. Create the file lib/dungeon_crawl/cli/room_actions_choice.ex and write the following module in it:

design_your_application/tutorial/0/dungeon_crawl/lib/dungeon_crawl/cli/room_actions_choice.ex

```elixir
defmodule DungeonCrawl.CLI.RoomActionsChoice do
  alias Mix.Shell.IO, as: Shell
  import DungeonCrawl.CLI.BaseCommands

  def start(room) do
    room_actions = room.actions
    find_action_by_index = &(Enum.at(room_actions, &1))

    Shell.info(room.description())

    chosen_action =
      room_actions
      |> Enum.map(&(&1.label))
      |> display_options
      |> generate_question
      |> Shell.prompt
      |> parse_answer
      |> find_action_by_index.()

    {room, chosen_action}
  end
end
```

The pipeline of functions is very similar to HeroChoice. The main difference here is the code that handles different structures of the room and its actions; also, we don't need to confirm what the player has chosen. The function returns a tuple with the room and the selected action. Now we can update our Dungeon-Crawl.CLI.Main module to call the action-selection function:

design_your_application/tutorial/2/dungeon_crawl/lib/dungeon_crawl/cli/main.ex

```elixir
def start_game do
  welcome_message()
  Shell.prompt("Press Enter to continue")
  hero_choice()
  crawl(DungeonCrawl.Room.all())
end

defp crawl(rooms) do
  Shell.info("You keep moving forward to the next room.")
  Shell.prompt("Press Enter to continue")
  Shell.cmd("clear")

  rooms
  |> Enum.random
  |> DungeonCrawl.CLI.RoomActionsChoice.start
end
```

The crawl/1 function expects a list of rooms. It takes a random room from the list and starts the action-selection interaction. You can see what's happening by running mix start.

❮ You keep moving forward to the next room.
Press Enter to continue

You found a quiet place. Looks safe for a little nap.
1 - Move forward
2 - Take a better look and rest
Which one? [1,2]
⇒ **1**

In RoomActionsChoice we reused some functions that we created in HeroChoice, reducing the code and creating this functionality more quickly.

## Displaying Heroes and Room Actions with Protocols

We listed the options for the player; these options can be room actions or heroes. It means we need to work with different data types, the DungeonCrawl.Character and DungeonCrawl.Room.Action structs. Handling different data structures with different attributes can be hard, making you create conditionals that are difficult to follow. We mapped the attributes before displaying them, and it was a good solution. Now we'll create an alternative solution that takes advantage of polymorphism. We'll make a display function that works with the DungeonCrawl.Character and DungeonCrawl.Room.Action structs. In Elixir we can create polymorphic functions using protocols. In this section you'll learn how to build your own protocol and implement existing ones.

We want to create a single function that doesn't care if you pass an action or a hero. Let's build the protocol for it in lib/dungeon_crawl/display.ex:

design_your_application/dungeon_crawl/lib/dungeon_crawl/display.ex
```
defprotocol DungeonCrawl.Display do
  def info(value)
end
```

It's very simple to define a protocol. We use the defprotocol directive, and then we create a function with def but without defining its body. Then our Dungeon-Crawl.Display protocol has one function called info/1. To make it work, we need to implement the protocol for the data types we want. Let's do it in the same file we were using:

design_your_application/dungeon_crawl/lib/dungeon_crawl/display.ex
```
defimpl DungeonCrawl.Display, for: DungeonCrawl.Room.Action do
  def info(action), do: action.label
end

defimpl DungeonCrawl.Display, for: DungeonCrawl.Character do
  def info(character), do: character.name
end
```

We implemented the protocol with the directive defimpl. We used the for option to specify the data type. Then, inside the directive body, we implemented the info/1 function. With this change, we can use DungeonCrawl.Display.info/1 with any of the implemented types. We added this extension without touching the data type modules. Protocols are very extensible. Let's update our Dungeon-Crawl.CLI.BaseCommands:

```
design_your_application/dungeon_crawl/lib/dungeon_crawl/cli/base_commands.ex
def display_options(options) do
  options
  |> Enum.with_index(1)
  |> Enum.each(fn {option, index} ->
    Shell.info("#{index} - #{DungeonCrawl.Display.info(option)}")
  end)

  options
end
```

Then we can remove the mapping attribute line with Enum.map/2 of Dungeon-Crawl.CLI.HeroChoice and DungeonCrawl.CLI.RoomActionsChoice:

```
design_your_application/tutorial/3/dungeon_crawl/lib/dungeon_crawl/cli/hero_choice.ex
heroes
|> display_options
```

```
design_your_application/tutorial/3/dungeon_crawl/lib/dungeon_crawl/cli/room_actions_choice.ex
room_actions
|> display_options
```

We're passing the data types directly, with no previous transformation, to display_options/1. Then display_options/1 will invoke DungeonCrawl.Display.info/1 to show the information. You can run mix start to see the update working.

We're using DungeonCrawl.DungeonCrawl.Display.info/1, and it's a little bit verbose. What if we could display the character or the room action with the Elixir conventional interpolation syntax? For example, if we write "1 - #{character}" and it displays the character name instead of the entire structure, it would be interesting, right? Elixir has the String.Chars protocol that enables it. We only need to implement the to_string/1 function. Let's do that in the modules DungeonCrawl.Character and DungeonCrawl.Room.Action:

```
design_your_application/dungeon_crawl/lib/dungeon_crawl/character.ex
defimpl String.Chars do
  def to_string(character), do: character.name
end
```

design_your_application/dungeon_crawl/lib/dungeon_crawl/room/action.ex

```elixir
defimpl String.Chars do
  def to_string(action), do: action.label
end
```

We don't need to use the option for to specify a module here because we're implementing a protocol inside of a module. Elixir understands that implementation is for the current module. You can remove the DungeonCrawl.DungeonCrawl.Display protocol since we won't use that anymore. Now we can update DungeonCrawl.CLI.BaseCommands.display_options/1 to use the string interpolation:

design_your_application/tutorial/1/dungeon_crawl/lib/dungeon_crawl/cli/base_commands.ex

```elixir
def display_options(options) do
  options
  |> Enum.with_index(1)
  |> Enum.each(fn {option, index} ->
    Shell.info("#{index} - #{option}")
  end)

  options
end
```

You can run mix start, and you'll see everything working. Elixir's protocols allow the code that uses the interface to stay the same when new data types are added. If you want to learn more about protocols and their options, take a look at the Elixir official guide.[4]

### Organizing Your Protocols

Here's the convention for protocol code organization: If you own the struct, put the implementation in the same file as the struct. If you don't own the struct but you own the protocol, put the implementation inside of the protocol file. If you own neither the struct nor the protocol, create a file with the protocol name and put the implementation there.

You've learned how to create complex data structures by using structs that reference other structs. You've learned to build a module with reusable functions by refactoring existing code. Finally, you've learned how to extend existing polymorphic functions and build new ones. However, it's not enough; protocols are good for structs but not for simple modules. In the next section you'll learn how to create interfaces for modules.

---

4. http://elixir-lang.org/getting-started/protocols.html

# Creating Module Behaviours

A contract sets the rules in an agreement between parties, and indicates how the parties will benefit. For example, think of a job contract. It has rules for the employee and the employer, and by following those rules both parties will reap specific benefits. If the rules are broken, though, those benefits aren't guaranteed. In Elixir, a *behaviour* is a contract between a module and the client code that's using it. It provides a common interface for a client across multiple modules. It means a client can use multiple modules in the same way since the modules provide the same functions with the same signatures defined in the behaviour contract. For example, Mix.Task is a behaviour. When we create a module that follows the Mix.Task behaviour, we must implement the function run/1. If we don't, Mix will have problems when trying to run our module as a task. It's very useful to enforce the practice of developers creating consistent code when developing new features in an application.

In this section you'll learn how to build your own behaviours. You'll learn to create better function signatures with type specifications. You'll see how to add a new library in your application. In the end, you'll learn how to use *Dialyzer* to check if your code has hidden bugs.

## Building the Exit with Elixir Behaviour

Let's return to our game example. The hero can walk for several rooms. Each room has a list of actions. The player chooses one action, and it will trigger a situation. Each situation can be very different, but it'd be nice if the situation triggers had uniform input and output. Having multiple functions that respect the same *behaviour* permits us to have a central point of execution and handling, avoiding extra conditional code.

For each type of room, we'll build a module. Inside each module we'll have the function that knows what to do when the user chooses an action for that room. The function must accept the hero and the player action as an argument and must return the hero with a flag. When the flag is :exit, the game is finished; when it's :forward, the hero must keep crawling the dungeon. We'll use an Elixir behaviour feature that will be like a simple contract of how that function should work. Create the file lib/dungeon_crawl/room/trigger.ex and write this module in it:

design_your_application/tutorial/0/dungeon_crawl/lib/dungeon_crawl/room/trigger.ex

```
defmodule DungeonCrawl.Room.Trigger do
  @callback run(character :: any, action :: any) :: any
end
```

We've used the @callback directive to tell Elixir we want to define a function rule. The syntax is very similar to how we create functions. We have the function called run. It must have two arguments; we'll use character and action. After the argument name we have the two colons, ::, with the word any indicating the arguments can be of any type. Then, after the function declaration we have the :: again. It defines the function type return; again we're using any. With this line we're saying any module that obeys this contract must have a function called run that has two arguments of any type, and returns a value of any type. I know it's not a strict contract, but it's enough to create our first room trigger.

Let's build the exit-room trigger. When a hero enters this room, nothing happens to the character and we return the exit flag. Create the lib/dungeon_crawl/room/triggers/exit.ex file with the following module:

```
design_your_application/tutorial/0/dungeon_crawl/lib/dungeon_crawl/room/triggers/exit.ex
defmodule DungeonCrawl.Room.Triggers.Exit do
  @behaviour DungeonCrawl.Room.Trigger
end
```

In this module we've used the @behaviour directive to tell Elixir the Exit module follows the Room.Trigger contract. That contract says we need to implement a run function. If we try to compile the project without implementing a run, the compiler will complain about the missing function. Try to run mix and see the error message:

```
$ mix
Compiling 1 file (.ex)
warning: undefined behaviour function run/2
  (for behaviour DungeonCrawl.Room.Trigger)
  lib/dungeon_crawl/room/triggers/exit.ex:1
```

It's very useful to alert developers about missing functions. Now let's implement the run/2 function:

```
design_your_application/dungeon_crawl/lib/dungeon_crawl/room/triggers/exit.ex
defmodule DungeonCrawl.Room.Triggers.Exit do
  @behaviour DungeonCrawl.Room.Trigger
  def run(character, _), do: {character, :exit}
end
```

The function is very simple. It returns a tuple with the given hero and a flag saying that character has found the exit. The next step is to build a room that contains the exit trigger. Let's update our DungeonCrawl.Room module:

```
design_your_application/tutorial/1/dungeon_crawl/lib/dungeon_crawl/room.ex
defmodule DungeonCrawl.Room do
  alias DungeonCrawl.Room
➤ alias DungeonCrawl.Room.Triggers

  import DungeonCrawl.Room.Action

➤ defstruct description: nil, actions: [], trigger: nil

  def all, do: [
    %Room{
➤     description: "You can see the light of day. You found the exit!",
➤     actions: [forward()],
➤     trigger: Triggers.Exit
    },
  ]
end
```

We've added an alias for DungeonCrawl.Room.Triggers to simplify the use of the room triggers in our module. We've added the trigger attribute to our room struct. It will store a module that respects the Room.Trigger contract, having the actions' behavior and consequences. Then in the all/0 function we create a room that has the exit trigger. Now we need to update the DungeonCrawl.CLI.Main to run the trigger when the player chooses an option. First, the crawl function must have a hero in the parameter:

```
design_your_application/tutorial/3/dungeon_crawl/lib/dungeon_crawl/cli/main.ex
def start_game do
  welcome_message()
  Shell.prompt("Press Enter to continue")

➤ crawl(hero_choice(), DungeonCrawl.Room.all())
end

➤ defp crawl(character, rooms) do
  Shell.info("You keep moving forward to the next room.")
  Shell.prompt("Press Enter to continue")
  Shell.cmd("clear")

  rooms
  |> Enum.random
  |> DungeonCrawl.CLI.RoomActionsChoice.start
➤ |> trigger_action(character)
➤ |> handle_action_result
end
```

The hero is now in the crawl arguments because it will be helpful to update the hero's health based on actions triggered in the room. Now let's add two new auxiliary functions—one to run the trigger and another to handle the result of the trigger:

design_your_application/tutorial/3/dungeon_crawl/lib/dungeon_crawl/cli/main.ex

```elixir
defp trigger_action({room, action}, character) do
  Shell.cmd("clear")
  room.trigger.run(character, action)
end

defp handle_action_result({_, :exit}),
  do: Shell.info("You found the exit. You won the game. Congratulations!")
defp handle_action_result({character, _}),
  do: crawl(character, DungeonCrawl.Room.all())
```

The trigger_action/2 is very simple: it clears the screen and invokes the function run/2 from the module that is stored in trigger attribute. The handle_action_result/2 function, when it matches the :exit flag, will finish the game. Otherwise it starts a recursive call to crawl/2, passing the hero and the rooms. With this change, we can run mix start and see the updates in our game:

```
You can see the light of day ahead. You found the exit!
1 - Move forward
Which one? [1]
1

You found the exit. You won the game. Congratulations!
```

We've finished an important part of the game. It now has a beginning and an end. We've used the behaviour feature to simplify the way developers implement new challenges in the game. They can add new room-trigger modules and respect the Room.Trigger contract. The next step is to improve it with *type specifications*, or *typespecs*.

## Adding Type Specifications

Type specifications are notations that say what your functions expect and return. In some languages the compiler uses the type specifications to optimize the code and check its correctness. Elixir is a dynamic language, and the compiler doesn't use type specifications to optimize our code. However, the Dialyzer tool uses type specifications to do a static check to verify if type usage is correct, catching some hidden bugs. Type specifications are also good for generating documentation, clarifying what is expected in our code. We'll use type specifications to improve the DungeonCrawl.Room.Trigger.run/2 contract, and we'll add them to document the expected structures in the function's arguments and return.

The DungeonCrawl.Room.Trigger.run/2 needs a character and a room action. We need to create the character and room types. Then we can specify the run/2 function's arguments. Let's define the character type in lib/dungeon_crawl/character.ex, adding the following code:

```
design_your_application/tutorial/1/dungeon_crawl/lib/dungeon_crawl/character.ex
@type t :: %DungeonCrawl.Character{
  name: String.t,
  description: String.t,
  hit_points: non_neg_integer,
  max_hit_points: non_neg_integer,
  attack_description: String.t,
  damage_range: Range.t
}
```

We used the @type directive to start the type definition. That type has the name t, and the code after the :: is the type definition. We're saying the type is a DungeonCrawl.Character struct, and is composed of attributes with their specified types. Some types we can reference with simple names, like integer. Types like String we reference by accessing the t function from their modules. It's a common convention in Elixir to define the struct type with t. With the type specification, it's way more clear what is expected in each attribute of the struct. The next step is to define the type specification of the room action:

```
design_your_application/dungeon_crawl/lib/dungeon_crawl/room/action.ex
@type t :: %Action{id: atom, label: String.t}
```

The id of the room should be an atom and the label should be a string. Then, finally, we improve our run/2 specification by associating the types that we created:

```
design_your_application/dungeon_crawl/lib/dungeon_crawl/room/trigger.ex
defmodule DungeonCrawl.Room.Trigger do
  alias DungeonCrawl.Character
  alias DungeonCrawl.Room.Action

➤  @callback run(Character.t, Action.t) :: {Character.t, atom}
end
```

In the first argument we expect a character type, and in the second we expect a room action type. The function is expected to return a tuple, where the first item is a character type and the second item is an atom. With this change, we have a clear rule for what run/2 expects and returns.

Type specifications are not just documentation for developers. You can use a tool that statically analyzes your code, checking that you didn't call a function passing the wrong type. Erlang's Dialyzer tool can be used in Elixir. We have the Dialyxir library that wraps Dialyzer, providing a default configuration and useful Mix tasks.[5]

To install Dialyxir, we need to add a library to our application. Mix provides an easy way of doing it. We need to update our library dependencies in mix.exs

---

5.   https://github.com/jeremyjh/dialyxir

and run some Mix tasks, and Mix will do the job for us. Update mix.exs with the following code:

```
defp deps do
  [
    {:dialyxir, "~> 0.5", only: [:dev], runtime: false},
  ]
end
```

In the deps function we must return a list of tuples. The first item is the name of the library, the second item is the version, and the third is an optional list of keyword options. We're saying here that we have the dialyxir library, the version must be >= 0.5.0 and < 1.0.0, and we only need it in the dev environment. The version scheme follows semantic versioning.[6] Now we need to run the tasks to download and compile this new library. The libraries for Elixir and Erlang are available online in Hex.[7] The Mix tasks will download the libraries from Hex. Run the following command:

```
$ mix do deps.get, deps.compile
Running dependency resolution...
Dependency resolution completed:
  dialyxir 0.5.0
* Getting dialyxir (Hex package)
  Checking package (https://repo.hex.pm/tarballs/dialyxir-0.5.0.tar)
  Fetched package
==> dialyxir
Compiling 5 files (.ex)
Generated dialyxir app
```

We've run multiple tasks with mix do—deps.get downloads the dependencies and deps.compile compiles them. After running these commands, the dialyzer task will be available for us to run in the terminal. When you run it initially, it will take a long time because it analyzes all of Elixir's language and libraries, then finally examines your code. The good part is that it caches the analysis to reuse in future runs, so it gets a lot faster. Run it:

```
$ mix dialyzer
# ...
:0: Unknown function 'Elixir.Mix.Shell.IO':cmd/1
:0: Unknown function 'Elixir.Mix.Shell.IO':info/1
:0: Unknown function 'Elixir.Mix.Shell.IO':prompt/1
:0: Unknown function 'Elixir.Mix.Shell.IO':'yes?'/1
lib/mix/tasks/start.ex:1: Callback info about the 'Elixir.Mix.Task' behaviour
is not available
```

---

6.   http://semver.org

7.   https://hex.pm

After a long run, you'll see Dialyzer complaining about Mix missing functions. Note: if you didn't remove the protocol DungeonCrawl.DungeonCrawl.Display you may see Dialyzer warnings about missing implementations. You can remove the protocol to fix the warning messages or just ignore them since the protocol implementations aren't mandatory. It can easily be fixed by telling Dialyzer to include Mix in the analysis. Change this line in your mix.exs file:

design_your_application/dungeon_crawl/mix.exs

```
def project do
  [app: :dungeon_crawl,
   version: "0.1.0",
   elixir: "~> 1.5",
   build_embedded: Mix.env == :prod,
   start_permanent: Mix.env == :prod,
   deps: deps(),
   dialyzer: [plt_add_apps: [:mix]]]
end
```

Run the Dialyzer again, and you'll see it stops complaining. To see it in action with your application code, try to make DungeonCrawl.Room.Trigger.Exit return a string instead of an atom. Then run it again, and it'll show a result similar to the output here:

```
$ mix dialyzer
lib/dungeon_crawl/room/triggers/exit.ex:3: The inferred return type of run/2
({_,<<_:32>>}) has nothing in common with
{#{'__struct__':='Elixir.DungeonCrawl.Character',
'attack_description':=binary(), 'damage_range':=#{'__struct__':='Elixir.Range',
'first':=integer(), 'last':=integer()}, 'description':=binary(),
'hit_points':=integer(), 'max_hit_points':=integer(),
'name':=binary()},atom()}, which is the expected return type for the callback
of 'Elixir.DungeonCrawl.Room.Trigger' behaviour
```

It will complain that your run/2 function doesn't respect the Elixir.DungeonCrawl.Room.Trigger behaviour. Typespecs aren't just used to document your functions, structs, and behaviours. They can be used to catch some bugs before you run your application in production with the dialyzer. If you want to learn more about typespecs, read the official Elixir documentation with the full list of built-in types and options.[8] Now we need to finish the game by developing a way the player can lose. In the next section, we'll implement a new room trigger using the behaviour that we created in this section.

## Battling Through to the Exit

Our game needs a challenge, or it won't be fun. A challenge will reduce the chances of the player winning. We'll implement a room with an enemy. The

---

8. https://hexdocs.pm/elixir/typespecs.html

hero and the enemy will fight, and the first one to reach zero hit points is defeated. We need to build a list of enemies, create functions to reduce and restore character hit points, build a battle module, and create a room that can trigger a battle. Once we have a room-trigger contract, we need to strictly follow it. The first step will be to construct a list of enemies, creating the lib/dungeon_crawl/enemies.ex file with the following code:

```
design_your_application/dungeon_crawl/lib/dungeon_crawl/enemies.ex
defmodule DungeonCrawl.Enemies do
  alias DungeonCrawl.Character

  def all, do: [
    %Character{
      name: "Ogre",
      description: "A large creature. Big muscles. Angry and hungry.",
      hit_points: 12,
      max_hit_points: 12,
      damage_range: 3..5,
      attack_description: "a hammer"
    },
    %Character{
      name: "Orc",
      description: "A green evil creature. Wears armor and an axe.",
      hit_points: 8,
      max_hit_points: 8,
      damage_range: 2..4,
      attack_description: "an axe"
    },
    %Character{
      name: "Goblin",
      description: "A small green creature. Wears dirty clothes and a dagger.",
      hit_points: 4,
      max_hit_points: 4,
      damage_range: 1..2,
      attack_description: "a dagger"
    },
  ]
end
```

We've used the same DungeonCrawl.Character struct of the hero to create the enemies. (It's a list of suggested enemies. Feel free to create more or change the list.) The next step is to create functions that permit reduction or restoration of a character's hit points, and another function that displays the character's current hit points. Write these functions in your DungeonCrawl.Character module:

```
design_your_application/dungeon_crawl/lib/dungeon_crawl/character.ex
def take_damage(character, damage) do
  new_hit_points = max(0, character.hit_points - damage)
  %{character | hit_points: new_hit_points}
end

def heal(character, healing_value) do
  new_hit_points = min(
    character.hit_points + healing_value,
    character.max_hit_points
  )
  %{character | hit_points: new_hit_points}
end

def current_stats(character),
  do: "Player Stats\nHP: #{character.hit_points}/#{character.max_hit_points}"
```

take_damage/2 receives a character and the number of hit points that character
should lose. The function won't let the character have negative hit points, so
it uses the function max to guarantee the character has at least zero hit points.
We're using the %{ map | key: new_value } syntax to update the values of the struct;
it's a handy Elixir shortcut. The function returns an updated character with
the new hit-points value. heal/2 receives a character and the number of hit
points that character should have restored. We use the min/2 function to
guarantee the hit points aren't greater than the character's maximum allowable
hit points. It returns an updated character with the new hit-points value.
current_stats/1 builds a message with the hero's current hit points compared to
the maximum allowable.

The battle module will have functions that will make two characters fight. It
doesn't matter if they're heroes or enemies; it will make each one attack the
other until one of them reaches zero hit points. Create lib/dungeon_crawl/battle.ex
and write the following module:

```
design_your_application/dungeon_crawl/lib/dungeon_crawl/battle.ex
defmodule DungeonCrawl.Battle do
  alias DungeonCrawl.Character
  alias Mix.Shell.IO, as: Shell

  def fight(
    char_a = %{hit_points: hit_points_a},
    char_b = %{hit_points: hit_points_b}
  ) when hit_points_a == 0 or hit_points_b == 0, do: {char_a, char_b}
  def fight(char_a, char_b) do
    char_b_after_damage = attack(char_a, char_b)
    char_a_after_damage = attack(char_b_after_damage, char_a)
    fight(char_a_after_damage, char_b_after_damage)
  end
```

```elixir
  defp attack(%{hit_points: hit_points_a}, character_b)
    when hit_points_a == 0, do: character_b
  defp attack(char_a, char_b) do
    damage = Enum.random(char_a.damage_range)
    char_b_after_damage = Character.take_damage(char_b, damage)

    char_a
      |> attack_message(damage)
      |> Shell.info

    char_b_after_damage
      |> receive_message(damage)
      |> Shell.info

    char_b_after_damage
  end

  defp attack_message(character = %{name: "You"}, damage) do
    "You attack with #{character.attack_description} " <>
    "and deal #{damage} damage."
  end
  defp attack_message(character, damage) do
    "#{character.name} attacks with " <>
    "#{character.attack_description} and " <>
    "deals #{damage} damage."
  end

  defp receive_message(character = %{name: "You"}, damage) do
    "You receive #{damage}. Current HP: #{character.hit_points}."
  end
  defp receive_message(character, damage) do
    "#{character.name} receives #{damage}. " <>
    "Current HP: #{character.hit_points}."
  end
end
```

The function fight/2 has to check if one of the characters has zero hit points. If yes, the battle is over and the function returns a tuple with the characters in the same order as the given arguments. If not, the characters will attack each other using the attack function. The function checks if the attacker has zero hit points; if so, nothing happens to the attacked character. If not, the attacked character receives a random amount of damage from the attacker's damage range. This function also prints on the console the damage taken and the current character hit points with the functions attack_message and receive_message. The message functions apply the proper grammar depending on whether the message is about the enemy or the player. Now let's build a room trigger that can start a battle. Create the file lib/dungeon_crawl/room/triggers/enemy.ex:

design_your_application/dungeon_crawl/lib/dungeon_crawl/room/triggers/enemy.ex

```elixir
defmodule DungeonCrawl.Room.Triggers.Enemy do
  @behaviour DungeonCrawl.Room.Trigger

  alias Mix.Shell.IO, as: Shell

  def run(character, %DungeonCrawl.Room.Action{id: :forward}) do
    enemy = Enum.random(DungeonCrawl.Enemies.all)

    Shell.info(enemy.description)
    Shell.info("The enemy #{enemy.name} wants to fight.")
    Shell.info("You were prepared and attack first.")
    {updated_char, _enemy} = DungeonCrawl.Battle.fight(character, enemy)

    {updated_char, :forward}
  end
end
```

The run/2 is simple. We take a random enemy from the list of enemies, and we invoke DungeonCrawl.Battle.fight/2, passing the hero and the enemy. The function's return is the updated character after the battle, and the flag forward indicates the player hasn't found the exit yet. Now we can create a new room and put it on the list with this trigger:

design_your_application/tutorial/2/dungeon_crawl/lib/dungeon_crawl/room.ex

```elixir
def all, do: [
  %Room{
    description: "You can see the light of day. You found the exit!",
    actions: [forward()],
    trigger: Triggers.Exit
  },
➤ %Room{
➤   description: "You can see an enemy blocking your path.",
➤   actions: [forward()],
➤   trigger: Triggers.Enemy
➤ },
]
```

Now the hero encounters an enemy in the dungeon. When the hero survives, he can keep crawling. However, when he reaches zero hit points, he can't keep crawling because he has too many wounds; it's game over—the player has lost. We need to update lib/dungeon_crawl/cli/main.ex with this new rule:

design_your_application/dungeon_crawl/lib/dungeon_crawl/cli/main.ex

```elixir
defp hero_choice do
➤ hero = DungeonCrawl.CLI.HeroChoice.start()
➤ %{hero | name: "You"}
  end

➤ defp crawl(%{hit_points: 0}, _) do
➤   Shell.prompt("")
➤   Shell.cmd("clear")
```

```
➤      Shell.info("Unfortunately your wounds are too many to keep walking.")
➤      Shell.info("You fall onto the floor without strength to carry on.")
➤      Shell.info("Game over!")
➤      Shell.prompt("")
➤    end

     defp crawl(character, rooms) do
       Shell.info("You keep moving forward to the next room.")
       Shell.prompt("Press Enter to continue")
       Shell.cmd("clear")

➤      Shell.info(DungeonCrawl.Character.current_stats(character))

       rooms
       |> Enum.random
       |> DungeonCrawl.CLI.RoomActionsChoice.start
       |> trigger_action(character)
       |> handle_action_result
     end
```

We've updated hero_choice/0 to change the chosen hero name to you, providing greater immersion for the player. We display the hero's current hit points before the player chooses an action; this way the player can better decide what to do. We created the crawl/2 clause, which shows a "game over" message and ends the game when the character reaches zero hit points. You can now run mix start to see the updates in the game. With luck, you'll fight an enemy and survive.

```
A large monster. Big muscles. Angry and hungry.
The enemy Ogre wants to fight.
You were prepared and attack first.
You attack with a fireball and deal 7 damage
Ogre receives 7. Current HP: 5.
Ogre attacks with a hammer and deals 4 damage
You receive 4. Current HP: 4.
You attack with a fireball and deal 10 damage
Ogre receives 10. Current HP: 0.
You keep moving forward to the next room.
Press Enter to continue
```

### Protocols vs. Behaviours

A quick comparison of protocols and behaviours: Protocols work with structs, and behaviours work with modules. Protocols create a function interface to work with several data types. Behaviours define a list of functions that a module should implement.

We've finished setting up how the game can end: the player wins or loses. You've learned how to build module contracts using Elixir's behaviours, making explicit how to add new modules to make the game more challenging.

You've seen how to add typespecs and analyze your code with Dialyzer to catch hidden bugs. You've added new libraries in your application, learning how to have new features without coding them yourself.

If you want to add more dungeon rooms, take a look at Appendix 1, *Adding Rooms to the Game*, on page 161. There you'll see some ideas to improve your game, like a trap room that damages players if they try to search for treasure.

# Wrapping Up

That was a challenging chapter! We've used everything we covered in the previous chapters to build a larger application, and we faced some new concepts. Let's review:

- We covered how to start a project with Mix and its basic commands.
- We saw how to structure the project in folders and namespaces.
- We created customized structs to describe our domain.
- We used Elixir protocols to achieve polymorphism.
- We used Elixir behaviours to create a contract between modules.

In the next chapter, the final chapter, we'll explore a topic that we ignored in this chapter: what to do when things don't work as expected. You'll learn how to handle errors and unexpected events.

## Your Turn

This time you won't have exercises with a right or wrong answer. Instead you'll have ideas to improve your game. You'll need to find your way; you must analyze trade-offs and decide on the solution you'll implement. Don't be afraid to rewrite some part of the game to accommodate changes and improvements. It's your game, so don't limit yourself to the ideas here!

- In the current game all the rooms have the same chance of appearing. That means the exit room might show up immediately, leading to a very short and dull game. Make it so certain rooms have a greater probability of showing up than others do.

- Add an extra option at the beginning of the game to allow players to choose the difficulty level. For example, when the player wants the game to be hard, the exit and healing rooms will be difficult to find.

- Implement a feature that changes the probability of the exit room appearing based on how many places the hero has visited. For example, at the beginning of the game the exit room will have no probability of appearing, but after some certain number of rounds, the chances of it appearing increase.

• Implement a scoring system. When the hero survives traps, defeats enemies, or finds treasures, the player's score will increase. When the player beats the game, the score is saved in a file. The file must contain only the top 10 scores.

• Make it so the hero can store items in his pocket to use later. For example, he can pick up the healing potion in the treasure room and use it later, when he's lost hit points. Add an option to use the item when listing room actions. It's good to indicate the maximum number of items the hero can accumulate.

• Improve the battle module by giving the player the option to run away or attack in that round. When the hero is fleeing, he'll receive one attack from the enemy before making his escape.

Additionally, Appendix 1, *Adding Rooms to the Game*, on page 161, contains more ideas you can implement to incorporate more dungeon rooms.

# CHAPTER 7

# Handling Impure Functions

The world is full of inconsistencies, and the resulting unpredictability is why we have impure functions—functions that can return different values from the same input. If you use a function that expects a number from users, what prevents them from inputting *hot dogs*? If you have a sign-in form on a website, what will prevent users from submitting the wrong password? If your program fetches data from a database, what guarantees that data is always there? Every program needs to handle errors and unexpected results. It's the programmer's job to code a friendly user experience in this wild world of events. While creating code for every uncertain possibility can be boring, working without any strategy will generate code that is hard to maintain. Real software must be reliable.

The main strategy for creating a healthy codebase is to identify and isolate the parts that can have unexpected results, and make them predictable. That way, the rest of the system can work with consistent values. In this chapter, we'll discuss and compare four strategies for doing this:

- Conditional structures: These are case, if, and similar statements.

- Elixir's try: Built for exception handling, this will be very familiar to people who come from C++, Ruby, or Java.

- Error monad: Monads are very common in functional languages that have static type systems.

- Elixir's with: This is a special directive that combines pattern matching with conditional execution.

You'll need the *dungeon crawl* application from Chapter 6, *Designing Your Elixir Applications*, on page 105, to experiment with the four strategies. If you know how to use a version-control system like Git, it's good to create branches before experimenting with each strategy. Then you'll have an easy way of navigating between and comparing the strategies. If you don't, you can copy and paste the project in different directories to experiment.

Our first step will not be a strategy. Instead, we will explore how to identify the functions that can have uncertain results in your program: the *impure* functions.

# Pure vs. Impure Functions

When we can't predict the results of a function, the function is impure. But before we can devise a strategy to handle impure functions, we need to know how to identify them. In this section you'll learn all the differences between predictable *pure functions* and unpredictable *impure functions*. In this book, you've seen many examples that contain impure and pure functions, but we didn't stop to understand their properties. Now the time has come. We'll explore them and understand how to identify them by writing some examples.

## Pure Functions

Pure functions always return consistent output when given the same input, and never produce effects beyond the function's scope, making them predictable. For example, write the following function that calculates the total from a given price and tax value:

```
iex> total = &(&1 * &2/100)
iex> total.(100, 8)
# => 8.0
iex> total.(100, 8)
# => 8.0
iex> total.(nil, 8)
** (ArithmeticError)
iex> total.(nil, 8)
** (ArithmeticError)
```

With a pure function, you can try total.(100, 8) a thousand times. No, wait. Try it a million times! You'll always see the same result (unless, of course, your computer is influenced by cosmic rays). If you try calculate_tax.(nil, 8), it always generates an error. Pure functions can result in errors, but the errors are predictable.

Pure functions are very predictable. They're so predictable that if you have your program call something like total.(100, 8), you can replace the entire function call with 8.0, and your program will work in the same way. It's called the *referential transparency* property of pure functions. Now that the definition of pure functions is clear, let's talk about impure functions.

## Impure Functions

Impure functions may not return consistent results when given the same inputs, and they may produce effects beyond the function's scope. That's why they're unpredictable. Let's experiment with one. In your IEx, try the following function:

```
iex> IO.gets "What's the meaning of life?\n"
```

You can type 42 and press `Enter`, and the result will be "42\n". Now you call IO.gets/1, passing "What's the meaning of life?\n" in the argument again. The program will ask again; type 43, press `Enter`, and the result will be "43\n". We've called a function with the same argument and it has resulted in different values. We have an impure function. Impure functions interact with content outside of the program context, such as when you read or write a file, access an API, fetch rows of a database, generate a random number, or ask for user input. The IO.gets/1 expects input from the terminal's user. We can't predict what the user will type; every time we call IO.gets/1, it can result in a different value.

And there's another definition of impure functions: a function is impure when it references values that aren't in the function arguments. If a function uses values outside of the function scope, it becomes impure. Let's see a practical example. Analyze this function:

```
iex> DateTime.utc_now()
%DateTime{calendar: Calendar.ISO, day: 5, hour: 1, microsecond: {961183, 6},
 minute: 17, month: 5, second: 2, std_offset: 0, time_zone: "Etc/UTC",
 utc_offset: 0, year: 2017, zone_abbr: "UTC"}
iex> DateTime.utc_now()
%DateTime{calendar: Calendar.ISO, day: 5, hour: 1, microsecond: {106169, 6},
 minute: 18, month: 5, second: 5, std_offset: 0, time_zone: "Etc/UTC",
 utc_offset: 0, year: 2017, zone_abbr: "UTC"}
```

The DateTime.utc_now() function is impure because every time we call it a new result is returned. Internally it consults the global machine clock state. If we create functions that rely on the DateTime.utc_now/0 result, they'll become impure. Let's see another:

```
iex> tax = 10
iex> total = &(&1 * tax/100)
iex> total.(100)
10.0
iex> tax = 0.8
iex> total.(100)
10.0
```

The total function is an interesting case. It references the tax variable, which is not a local variable. tax is outside of the function scope; thus total is impure.

However, thanks to immutability, rebinding the tax variable doesn't affect the total function. The tax value for the total function is permanent, so every time we call the total, passing the same argument will result in a consistent value. Given that, is the total function pure or impure? What a dilemma! It's pure because its output is affected only by the input.

There's one last definition of impure functions: a function is impure when it produces side effects. Side effects involve value access or value manipulation that your function does outside of its scope. Side effects include writing messages in the terminal, changing the global state, inserting or fetching rows in a database, accessing an API, and so on. Consider the following function:

```
iex> total = fn val, tax -> total = val * tax/100; IO.puts(total); total end
iex> total.(100, 10)
10.0
10.0
iex> total.(100, 10)
10.0
10.0
```

The total function returns consistent results based on its arguments. However, it's printing a message using the IO module; that's a side effect. Functions with side effects are impure. Producing functions like this is a bad practice; another developer using this function would not expect that total prints messages in the console. In a scenario that doesn't have an IO device, this simple function will result in an unexpected error. It's better to limit the total function to calculation responsibilities, and move IO.puts/1 outside of total. Here's an example:

```
iex> total = &(&1 * &2/100)
iex> IO.puts(total.(100, 10))
10.0
```

That's one way we can isolate the impure functions from the pure ones: by moving and separating them. You shouldn't think impure functions are evil and pure functions are good. You need both to write useful software. Pure functions are simple to maintain because they are predictable. Impure functions are necessary to build useful software. In order to build maintainable software, you should produce more pure functions while isolating the impure parts with proper handling.

Now that you know how to identify impure functions, it's time to explore the strategies to isolate their effects. We'll look at how to make the functions more predictable, isolating the unexpected results so they don't propagate to the entire system. Let's start with conditional structures.

## Controlling the Flow of Impure Functions

The first strategy for handling unexpected events is to control the flow like we covered in Chapter 3, *Using Pattern Matching to Control the Program Flow*, on page 33. You can use conditional structures, like case, if, or function clauses, to handle impure function results. They are flexible and good for handling simple cases, but not so much for complex ones. Let's see how they do the job well:

handle_the_uncertain/case/0/shop.ex
```
defmodule Shop do
  def checkout(price) do
    case ask_number("Quantity?") do
      :error -> IO.puts("It's not a number")
      {quantity, _} -> quantity * price
    end
  end

  def ask_number(message) do
    message <> "\n"
      |> IO.gets
      |> Integer.parse
  end
end
```

In this example, the program asks the user to enter a number, and we use the function IO.gets/1 to get the user's input. We know IO.gets/1 is an impure function and it can return anything; for instance, "42\n" or "hot dogs\n". If it's not a number, parsing it with Integer.parse/1 can result in an error. We use case to check it with pattern matching. It's very simple and quick to use, but we can easily mess up the code when things get more complicated. For example, let's imagine we want to ask the price in addition to quantity and apply the same strategy.

handle_the_uncertain/case/1/shop.ex
```
def checkout() do
  case ask_number("Quantity?") do
    :error ->
      IO.puts("It's not a number")
    {quantity, _} ->
      case ask_number("Price?") do
        :error ->
          IO.puts("It's not a number")
        {price, _} ->
          quantity * price
      end
  end
end
```

You can see the ugly conditional nesting of applying the strategy again. It's hard to understand. We can reduce the ugliness by using functions:

```
handle_the_uncertain/case/2/shop.ex
def checkout() do
  quantity = ask_number("Quantity?")
  price = ask_number("Price?")
  calculate(quantity, price)
end

def calculate(:error, _), do: IO.puts("Quantity is not a number")
def calculate(_, :error), do: IO.puts("Price is not a number")
def calculate({quantity, _}, {price, _}), do: quantity * price
```

We've changed how checkout/0 works, using functions and pattern matching to show when the price or quantity is not a valid number. Now let's experiment with the conventional control-flow statements to handle the user input in our *dungeon crawl* application. In this application, the critical point of uncertain values is when we ask users to choose an option by typing a number. We have two possibilities of failure:

- Users can type "hot dogs", and it's not valid a number.
- If we have three options, users can type 9999. It's a valid number but is not a valid option. It's out of the possible values range.

If one of these things happens, our application will fail. Let's improve it, asking the user to try again when an invalid option is inputted. In the Dungeon-Crawl.CLI.BaseCommands modules, write the following functions:

```
handle_the_uncertain/case/dungeon_crawl/lib/dungeon_crawl/cli/base_commands.ex
def ask_for_index(options) do
  answer =
    options
    |> display_options
    |> generate_question
    |> Shell.prompt
    |> Integer.parse

  case answer do
    :error ->
      display_invalid_option()
      ask_for_index(options)
    {option, _} ->
      option - 1
  end
end

def display_invalid_option do
  Shell.cmd("clear")
  Shell.error("Invalid option.")
  Shell.prompt("Press Enter to try again.")
  Shell.cmd("clear")
end
```

In ask_for_index/1, we ask the user to input a number that will be used as an index to find the correct option. We use Integer.parse/1 and check with case if the user has typed a valid number. We display an error message with display_invalid_option/0 and make the user try again when the number is invalid. If the user inputs a valid number, we just return the number. Now we need to find the correct option given the index number. Write the following function:

handle_the_uncertain/case/dungeon_crawl/lib/dungeon_crawl/cli/base_commands.ex
```elixir
def ask_for_option(options) do
  index = ask_for_index(options)
  chosen_option = Enum.at(options, index)
  chosen_option
    || (display_invalid_option() && ask_for_option(options))
end
```

Using Enum.at/2 we try to find the option with the index input by the user. It returns nil when it doesn't find an existing index. Remember, the nil value is falsy. We return chose_option when it's truthy. When it's not, we use the operator || to display the invalid option message and ask the user to try again.

We'll refactor the code of DungeonCrawl.CLI.HeroChoice and DungeonCrawl.CLI.RoomActionsChoice to take advantage of the new DungeonCrawl.CLI.BaseCommands.ask_for_option/1 function. Update your modules with this:

handle_the_uncertain/case/dungeon_crawl/lib/dungeon_crawl/cli/hero_choice.ex
```elixir
defmodule DungeonCrawl.CLI.HeroChoice do
  alias Mix.Shell.IO, as: Shell
  import DungeonCrawl.CLI.BaseCommands

  def start do
    Shell.cmd("clear")
    Shell.info("Start by choosing your hero:")

    DungeonCrawl.Heroes.all()
    |> ask_for_option
    |> confirm_hero
  end

  defp confirm_hero(chosen_hero) do
    Shell.cmd("clear")
    Shell.info(chosen_hero.description)
    if Shell.yes?("Confirm?"), do: chosen_hero, else: start()
  end
end
```

handle_the_uncertain/case/dungeon_crawl/lib/dungeon_crawl/cli/room_actions_choice.ex
```elixir
defmodule DungeonCrawl.CLI.RoomActionsChoice do
  alias Mix.Shell.IO, as: Shell
  import DungeonCrawl.CLI.BaseCommands
```

```
  def start(room) do
    Shell.info(room.description())
    chosen_action = ask_for_option(room.actions)
    {room, chosen_action}
  end
end
```

This refactoring will be very useful for the strategies we'll experiment with. Each approach will refactor the internals of ask_for_option/1, letting us focus on one module. You can see the updates in the project by running mix start:

```
Start playing the game by choosing your hero:
1 - Knight
2 - Wizard
3 - Rogue
Which one? [1,2,3]
hot dogs

Invalid option
Press Enter to continue.

1 - Knight
2 - Wizard
3 - Rogue
Which one? [1,2,3]
```

We have used conventional control-flow statements; they're familiar to developers of any level, they're simple to build, and the functions always return a value. But it's hard to combine them with other functions, and the code can get complex easily. You can use conditional structures when you know the function is simple.

## Trying, Rescuing, and Catching

With some functions, you don't control the code—and it can raise errors or throw values. You need the try statement to handle the unexpected results. If you came from object-oriented languages like C++, Java, and Ruby, this technique will be familiar to you.

Most of the time you can easily identify the functions that can raise errors or throw values because their names end with an exclamation point. For example, the File.cd!/1 function raises an exception when the path doesn't exist.

try wraps a code block. If an error is raised, you can use rescue to recover. An error (or *exception*) in Elixir is a special data structure that describes when an exceptional thing happens in the code. You can also use try to capture values with catch, because functions in Elixir can stop their own execution by sending a value with the throw directive.

Throwing values or raising errors is unusual in functional programming. However, in large applications you'll install libraries from other developers that use this strategy, and you need to know how to properly handle the raised errors and thrown values. In this section we'll see the try, raise, and rescue combination for exceptions, and the try, throw, and catch combination for values. You'll learn how to apply and handle them.

## Try, Raise, and Rescue

In Elixir, functions can raise exceptions when they're in a situation that's very wrong—so wrong that they must stop the execution and show a stack trace. We'll see how to raise and rescue exceptions. Let's see how we can rescue an exception by rewriting the Shop module example:

handle_the_uncertain/tryrescue/shop.ex
```
def checkout() do
  try do
    {quantity, _} = ask_number("Quantity?")
    {price, _} = ask_number("Price?")
    quantity * price
  rescue
    MatchError -> "It's not a number"
  end
end
```

Inside the try block, we create the happy-path code. The happy path is the code that handles only the success scenario. Then, in the rescue block, we create the error-handling code. Still in the rescue block, for each line we should provide an exception struct to match, and a code block. When the pattern matching fails the MatchError exception will be raised, and then the list of pattern-matching expressions in the rescue will try to match the exception and execute the code block. If none of the pattern-matching expressions matches an exception raised, Elixir will raise that exception again.

Let's experiment with this strategy in the *dungeon crawl* application. We'll create an exception struct in lib/dungeon_crawl/cli/invalid_option.ex because rescuing the MatchError exception is not the best solution. MatchError is too generic; it can happen for several reasons. It's better to provide specific error structs to clarify the problem by adding more context:

handle_the_uncertain/tryrescue/dungeon_crawl/lib/dungeon_crawl/cli/invalid_option.ex
```
defmodule DungeonCrawl.CLI.InvalidOptionError do
  defexception message: "Invalid option"
end
```

We've used the directive defexception to create our exception struct. We provided a default error message using the option message: "Invalid option". You can see more details about the defexception function and the Exception behaviour in the Elixir official documentation.[1] Now we can raise this exception when the user enters an invalid number or an option that doesn't exist. Go to the Dungeon-Crawl.CLI.BaseCommands and write parse_answer/1 and find_option_by_index/2, like this:

handle_the_uncertain/tryrescue/dungeon_crawl/lib/dungeon_crawl/cli/base_commands.ex
```elixir
def parse_answer!(answer) do
  case Integer.parse(answer) do
    :error ->
      raise DungeonCrawl.CLI.InvalidOptionError
    {option, _} ->
      option - 1
  end
end

def find_option_by_index!(index, options) do
  Enum.at(options, index)
    || raise DungeonCrawl.CLI.InvalidOptionError
end
```

We're using the control-flow techniques to raise errors inside the functions parse_answer!/1 and find_option_by_index!/2. The raise function expects an exception structure. When raise is called, it stops the function's execution. If no rescue is used, the program stops showing the stack trace. Now let's write the ask_for_option/1 function that uses try and rescue:

handle_the_uncertain/tryrescue/dungeon_crawl/lib/dungeon_crawl/cli/base_commands.ex
```elixir
def ask_for_option(options) do
  try do
    options
    |> display_options
    |> generate_question
    |> Shell.prompt
    |> parse_answer!
    |> find_option_by_index!(options)
  rescue
    e in DungeonCrawl.CLI.InvalidOptionError ->
      display_error(e)
      ask_for_option(options)
  end
end

def display_error(e) do
  Shell.cmd("clear")
  Shell.error(e.message)
  Shell.prompt("Press Enter to continue.")
  Shell.cmd("clear")
end
```

---

1.  https://hexdocs.pm/elixir/Kernel.html#defexception/1

In the try code block, we created the happy path of the pipeline of functions. In the rescue block we matched DungeonCrawl.CLI.InvalidOptionError and put the struct in a variable e. We used the display_error/1 function to show the error message. We also forced the user to try again, making a recursive call. You can run mix start and see the updates; it should work like before.

## Try, Throw, and Catch

throw and catch are very similar to raise and rescue. The main difference is that the throw/catch combination does not necessarily mean an error. It will stop the function from throwing a value that must be caught; it works like a control-flow structure. Let's experiment with it in our code. First, instead of raise an exception, we'll throw a value:

handle_the_uncertain/trycatch/dungeon_crawl/lib/dungeon_crawl/cli/base_commands.ex
```
@invalid_option {:error, "Invalid option"}

def parse_answer(answer) do
  case Integer.parse(answer) do
    :error ->
      throw @invalid_option
    {option, _} ->
      option - 1
  end
end

def find_option_by_index(index, options) do
  Enum.at(options, index) || throw @invalid_option
end
```

We created the tuple @invalid_option that contains an atom indicating an error, and a string with an error message. Then we used the function throw to stop the function execution from throwing the @invalid_option value when parse_answer/1 or find_option_by_index/2 results in an error. Now we need to catch the @invalid_option in ask_for_option/1.

handle_the_uncertain/trycatch/dungeon_crawl/lib/dungeon_crawl/cli/base_commands.ex
```
def ask_for_option(options) do
  try do
    options
    |> display_options
    |> generate_question
    |> Shell.prompt
    |> parse_answer
    |> find_option_by_index(options)
  catch
    {:error, message} ->
      display_error(message)
      ask_for_option(options)
  end
end
```

```
def display_error(message) do
  Shell.cmd("clear")
  Shell.error(message)
  Shell.prompt("Press Enter to continue.")
  Shell.cmd("clear")
end
```

This is very similar to how we used the try and rescue version. Inside the try block we have the happy-path code. In the catch block we used pattern matching to catch the values thrown. catch works very similarly to the case statement: each line has a pattern-matching expression and a code block to be executed.

If you only need one try block in your function, you can omit try do. Take a look:

```
handle_the_uncertain/trycatch/dungeon_crawl/lib/dungeon_crawl/cli/base_commands.ex
def ask_for_option(options) do
  options
  |> display_options
  |> generate_question
  |> Shell.prompt
  |> parse_answer
  |> find_option_by_index(options)
catch
  {:error, message} ->
    display_error(message)
    ask_for_option(options)
end
```

You can now see the updates by running mix start; everything should be working.

Using try offers a clear view of the function's happy path, but it also makes our functions harder to use because of the additional language features (catch, rescue, raise, and throw) to handle the exceptional results. Because of this additional complexity, Elixir developers tend to avoid the strategy of raising errors or throwing values. They prefer the alternative strategies that are described in this chapter. However, you may find some libraries that use this strategy, and you'll need to know how to handle them to create predictable code.

## Handling Impure Functions with the Error Monad

The Error monad is a data structure that helps you combine functions that can result in an error. It permits you to put functions into a clear sequence, handling the error at a unique point. It helps you reduce conditional codes when functions can have unexpected results. You should use it when your codebase is filled with situations where you must put many functions in sequence and some of them can fail. For example, maybe you have five functions that must be executed in sequence, but some of them are prone to failure.

You may have heard of *monads*—they are famous in languages with strong and static typing, such as Haskell. Monads have strong mathematical theory, and concepts like functors, applicatives, and monoids. But don't worry: we'll focus on how to use monads in practice.

In general, a monad wraps a value with properties that give more information about that value—they give the context. Having a value with context makes possible the process of combining functions with values to make automatic decisions. For example, if we have context for when a value is an error or a success, we can automatically skip function executions when the value is an error. Take a look at this example:

**Error Monad**

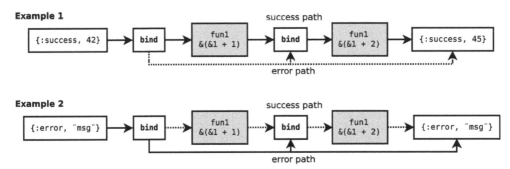

With the Error monad, we have an automatic decision of skipping function executions when the value has an error, bringing the failure handling to a central point. To make it work, we need to pass the monad with the value and the function to the bind function. The bind knows how to combine the function and the value. It invokes the function, passing the value extracted from the monad. The bind function knows to do any additional task that each monad type needs. In this example, when we bind data to a function with an Error monad, bind executes the function only if the data is marked as a success; when it's a failure, bind ignores the function invocation.

Let's experiment with the monad strategy in our *dungeon crawl* application. We aren't going to write a monad implementation from scratch. Instead, we'll use a community library. We have some options in Elixir, such as Monad,[2]

---

2.   https://github.com/rmies/monad

Towel,[3] witchcraft,[4] and MonadEx.[5] Each library has its merits and downsides; the choice here is very subjective. We'll use MonadEx because, today, it's the library that has the most stars, watchers, and forks on GitHub. The MonadEx README contains a lot of useful links to learn more about monads. Go to your mix.exs file and add MonadEx:

```
handle_the_uncertain/monad/dungeon_crawl/mix.exs
defp deps do
  [
    {:dialyxir, "~> 0.5", only: [:dev], runtime: false},
    {:monadex, "~> 1.1"}
  ]
end
```

Run the following command to install and compile the MonadEx library:

```
$ mix do deps.get, deps.compile
Running dependency resolution...
* Getting monadex (Hex package)
  Checking package (https://repo.hex.pm/tarballs/monadex-1.1.2.tar)
  Fetched package
==> monadex
Compiling 16 files (.ex)
Generated monadex app
```

The MonadEx library will be downloaded and compiled, making it ready to use in our application. Let's experiment with something similar to the scenario in the preceding image using our IEx. In your terminal, run iex -S mix and try it:

```
iex> use Monad.Operators
iex> import Monad.Result
iex> success(42) ~>> (& &1 + 1) ~>> (& &1 + 2)
45
iex> error("wrong") ~>> (& &1 + 1) ~>> (& &1 + 2)
%Monad.Result{error: "wrong", type: :error, value: nil}
```

We've employed the use Monad.Operators directive to add a ~>> operator—the *bind* operator—to our session. This operator is the bind function that we've discussed before. The left side expects a monad and the right side expects a function. We import the functions from Monad.Result. The Result monad is the same as the Error monad that we've discussed previously. (This library's author gave it a different name, but they are the same thing.) The success/1 function wraps the value in a success context and error/1 wraps the value in an error

---

3.   https://github.com/knrz/towel
4.   https://github.com/expede/witchcraft
5.   https://github.com/rob-brown/MonadEx

context. The ~>> operator executes values in a success context while skipping values in an error context.

Let's rewrite our DungeonCrawl.CLI.BaseCommands to experiment with the monad strategy. In the beginning of the module, we'll import some functions from MonadEx:

handle_the_uncertain/monad/dungeon_crawl/lib/dungeon_crawl/cli/base_commands.ex
```
use Monad.Operators

alias Mix.Shell.IO, as: Shell
import Monad.Result, only: [success: 1, success?: 1, error: 1, return: 1]
```

Here are the functions we've imported from Monad.Result:

- success/1, which wraps the given value in a result monad marked with success.

- return/1, which wraps the given value in a result monad marked with success.

- error/1, which wraps the given message in a result monad marked with failure.

- success?/1, which returns true when the given result monad is marked with success; otherwise it returns false.

success/1 and return/1 do the same thing. We have two names because sometimes it's more favorable semantically to use one over another. Now let's rewrite our base command functions to return monads:

handle_the_uncertain/monad/dungeon_crawl/lib/dungeon_crawl/cli/base_commands.ex
```
def display_options(options) do
  options
  |> Enum.with_index(1)
  |> Enum.each(fn {option, index} ->
    Shell.info("#{index} - #{option}")
  end)

  return(options)
end

def generate_question(options) do
  options = Enum.join(1..Enum.count(options),",")
  "Which one? [#{options}]\n"
end
```

In display_options/1 we use the function return to wrap the list of options in a success result. That's necessary because in this library lists are a type of monad. If we pass a list to the bind operator, it will try to extract the items of the list. We don't want an extraction in this case. That's why we wrap the list in a result monad. The generate_question/1 returns a string value. Using this library, it's optional to wrap a string value in a result monad. The bind function doesn't try to extract values that aren't monads. Change the following functions to return monads:

handle_the_uncertain/monad/dungeon_crawl/lib/dungeon_crawl/cli/base_commands.ex

```elixir
def parse_answer(answer) do
  case Integer.parse(answer) do
    :error -> error("Invalid option")
    {option, _} -> success(option - 1)
  end
end

def find_option_by_index(index, options) do
  case Enum.at(options, index) do
    nil -> error("Invalid option")
    chosen_option -> success(chosen_option)
  end
end
```

In parse_answer/1 the integer parsing can result in an error. We check it using case with pattern matching. When the parsed result is an error, we use error/1 to return an error result with a message. When the parsed result is a valid number, we use success/1 to return a success result wrapping the number. find_option_by_index/2 follows the same logic. When it matches a nil value we return an error result; when it matches a number we return a success result. After adapting our functions with monads, we can update ask_for_option/1 to take advantage of it:

handle_the_uncertain/monad/dungeon_crawl/lib/dungeon_crawl/cli/base_commands.ex

```elixir
def ask_for_option(options) do
  result =
    return(options)
      ~>> (&display_options/1)
      ~>> (&generate_question/1)
      ~>> (&Shell.prompt/1)
      ~>> (&parse_answer/1)
      ~>> (&(find_option_by_index(&1, options)))

  if success?(result) do
    result.value
  else
    display_error(result.error)
    ask_for_option(options)
  end
end
```

```
def display_error(message) do
  Shell.cmd("clear")
  Shell.error(message)
  Shell.prompt("Press Enter to continue.")
  Shell.cmd("clear")
end
```

We start the pipeline using the return/1 function to wrap the options list in a result monad. We need to do that because lists are monads and will trigger a different action in the bind operator. We use ~>>, the bind operator, to pipeline the functions. It works in a very similar way to our old friend the pipe operator, |>. The main difference here is that the right side of the ~>> expects an anonymous function. The ~>> will decide automatically whether it should execute the next function. If the value is marked with an error, ~>> skips the next function; if the value is marked with a success, ~>> will execute the next function. Thanks to this operator, we can create a clear function-execution sequence and handle the error after it rather than immediately when the error is happening.

We put the returning value of the pipeline execution in the result variable. We check if the result is a success with the success?/1 function. If it returns true we return the chosen option, accessing the value attribute. If it returns false we display the error and ask the user to try again. You can run mix start and see the application working with this new strategy.

We've used a monad to handle the invalid options. Here are the main advantages: We have a clear happy path of the function pipeline. We put the error handling at a unique point. The functions always return a value, returning a consistent data structure that flags an error or a success. There are also some disadvantages: Elixir doesn't have built-in support for monads, so we need to choose a library in the community. And the monad libraries may look disconnected from the rest of the language—for example, using anonymous functions with the ~>> operator is not clean like using the Elixir |> operator.

## Using with

Elixir's special form with permits you to combine multiple matching clauses. If all clauses match, the code executes and returns the do block result. If one clause doesn't match, the code stops and returns the value of the non-matching clause. It's useful to combine clauses that can result in unexpected values. Then you can handle the error at a convenient point, reducing the conditional code for each error. You should use with when you have function pipelines that can result in an error. We'll use with in the *dungeon crawl* application, but first let's try it in a simple example:

```
handle_the_uncertain/with/0/shop.ex
def checkout() do
  result =
    with {quantity, _} <- ask_number("Quantity?"),
         {price, _} <- ask_number("Price?"),
      do: quantity * price
  if result == :error, do: IO.puts("It's not a number"), else: result
end
```

We must put pattern-matching clauses inside the with clause; it's similar to how the case statement works. The big difference is the inversion of the execution highlighted by the <- operator . First, Elixir will execute the block on the right side of the operator. The pattern-matching on the left side of the <- operator will match the result of the block. When it matches, Elixir will execute the next instruction. You can add many instructions inside of with by separating them with commas. The final execution is determined by the keyword do. If one of the instructions doesn't have a match, Elixir will stop and return the unmatched value. Alternatively, we can use the else block of with to handle the values that didn't match. Here's an example:

```
handle_the_uncertain/with/1/shop.ex
def checkout() do
  with {quantity, _} <- ask_number("Quantity?"),
       {price, _} <- ask_number("Price?") do
    quantity * price
  else
    :error ->
      IO.puts("It's not a number")
  end
end
```

In the else block we can use the conventional pattern-matching clauses for values that didn't match in the with block. The value of the expression matched in the else block will be returned. An error is raised if a value doesn't match in either the with or the else block.

Let's apply with in our DungeonCrawl.CLI.BaseCommands. We can remove some functions since with is very flexible about matching the errors:

```
handle_the_uncertain/with/dungeon_crawl/lib/dungeon_crawl/cli/base_commands.ex
def display_options(options) do
  options
  |> Enum.with_index(1)
  |> Enum.each(fn {option, index} ->
    Shell.info("#{index} - #{option}")
  end)

  options
end
```

```
def generate_question(options) do
  options = Enum.join(1..Enum.count(options),",")
  "Which one? [#{options}]\n"
end
```

The with will require a different structure in our code. We removed the parse_answer/1 and find_option_by_index/2 functions because they won't be necessary any more. We let display_options/1 and generate_question/1 do the job like we did in previous chapters. We can write the ask_for_option/1 function using with:

handle_the_uncertain/with/dungeon_crawl/lib/dungeon_crawl/cli/base_commands.ex
```
def ask_for_option(options) do
  answer =
    options
    |> display_options
    |> generate_question
    |> Shell.prompt

  with {option, _} <- Integer.parse(answer),
       chosen when chosen != nil <- Enum.at(options, option - 1) do
    chosen
  else
    :error -> retry(options)
    nil -> retry(options)
  end
end

def retry(options) do
  display_error("Invalid option")
  ask_for_option(options)
end

def display_error(message) do
  Shell.cmd("clear")
  Shell.error(message)
  Shell.prompt("Press Enter to continue.")
  Shell.cmd("clear")
end
```

We can clearly see that the ask_for_option/1 function has three parts. In the first one we display options to the user and get an answer. In the second part we use with to parse and find the user's chosen option. In the third part we use the else block of with to handle invalid answers, asking the user to try again with the function retry. Note that we aren't using the wildcard operator to match both nil and :error. It's good to match the error explicitly so you'll always have a conscious decision about what to do when an error happens, avoiding unexpected results and hard-to-detect bugs.

The with statement combines expressions and handles their results. The advantage of this strategy is flexibility. Using with combined with pattern matching, we can check any value or pattern quickly and easily, without any new data structure, concepts, or libraries. The disadvantage of with is that it doesn't combine with the pipe operator, breaking the beautiful structure of the happy-path code.

# Wrapping Up

We've reached the end of the book. We've discussed the advantages and disadvantages of four strategies to handle uncertain values in functions. With this knowledge, you can promote changes in your codebase to achieve a low maintenance cost. Let's review what you've learned in this chapter:

- Impure functions can result in unexpected values because they depend on values that are not in the function's scope.

- case, if, and other control-flow statements are good for handling simple cases. Combining multiple conditional statements produces code that's hard to understand. You should avoid it.

- The try statement works with libraries where you don't control the code. These libraries can raise errors or throw values. Functions that return values are simpler and easier to handle than functions that raise errors or throw values. Thus, you should avoid creating functions that use raise and throw.

- You don't need to learn all the theory behind monads—nor have a mathematics degree—to start using simple monads like Error. It helps generate simple code and is easy to use. However, it's not part of the Elixir built-in ecosystem; the search for a library that fits your team's needs and tastes can be challenging.

- The with statement is very flexible for handling uncertain values thanks to pattern matching. It's the pragmatic strategy for most cases.

You've learned the final important concepts of functional programming. With all these concepts you're ready to build your own path to master functional programming with Elixir.

## Your Turn

In Chapter 6, *Designing Your Elixir Applications*, on page 105, we built the *dungeon crawl* application. A lot of functions in it are impure because of the IO operations. Review the *dungeon crawl* application: you'll see some parts that are mixing pure calculations with side effects and printing messages in the terminal. Can we separate the pure and impure parts of the code? There's no wrong or right answer; it's up to you decide the dissemination level of the impure functions.

## What's Next?

You finished the book! I hope you enjoyed this journey. We traveled together through many concepts in functional programming. We've seen a lot of features that make Elixir shine. Functional programming has helped me build better code in Elixir. And beyond Elixir, functional programming concepts have helped me write better code in Ruby and JavaScript. I'm sure you'll see the same result. With the knowledge you have now, I'm confident you'll be able to overcome all the challenges you'll face. Before we say goodbye, I have some recommendations to continue your journey.

- Have you liked Elixir? Do you want to learn more about it? *Programming Elixir 1.6 [Tho18]* will take you through all of Elixir's most important features for working with concurrent programming.

- Have you liked adding the use directive in your modules, giving them powerful features? It was built with Elixir metaprogramming. If you want to learn more about it, you can read *Metaprogramming Elixir [McC15]*.

- Are you a web developer? Do you want to build web applications using Elixir and functional programming? Take a look at *Programming Phoenix 1.3 [TV18]* and *Functional Web Development with Elixir, OTP, and Phoenix [Hal18]*.

- Elixir was built on top of the Erlang ecosystem. Why not dive in and learn some Erlang? *Programming Erlang (2nd edition) [Arm13]* will guide you.

No matter what path you choose next, just remember to have fun.

# Adding Rooms to the Game

A game where you only face an enemy and find an exit isn't that interesting. A game should have more challenges and places to explore. You can use your imagination to create additional interesting ideas for the game you built in Chapter 6, *Designing Your Elixir Applications*, on page 105. Here are some suggestions that you can implement in your game:

design_your_application/dungeon_crawl/lib/dungeon_crawl/room/triggers/trap.ex

```elixir
defmodule DungeonCrawl.Room.Triggers.Trap do
  alias DungeonCrawl.Room.Action
  alias Mix.Shell.IO, as: Shell

  @behaviour DungeonCrawl.Room.Trigger

  def run(character, %Action{id: :forward}) do
    Shell.info("You're walking cautiously and can see the next room.")
    {character, :forward}
  end
  def run(character, %Action{id: :search}) do
    damage = 3

    Shell.info("You search the room looking for something useful.")
    Shell.info("You step on a false floor and fall into a trap.")
    Shell.info("You are hit by an arrow, losing #{damage} hit points.")

    {
      DungeonCrawl.Character.take_damage(character, damage),
      :forward
    }
  end
end
```

The trap trigger works like this: if the player tries to search the room, she'll fall into a trap. When the clause matches, the :search action will make the hero lose hit points. We use DungeonCrawl.Character.take_damage/2 to reduce the hero's health. We can make a similar version of this trigger and create one that restores the hero's health:

design_your_application/dungeon_crawl/lib/dungeon_crawl/room/triggers/treasure.ex

```
defmodule DungeonCrawl.Room.Triggers.Treasure do
  alias DungeonCrawl.Room.Action
  alias Mix.Shell.IO, as: Shell

  @behaviour DungeonCrawl.Room.Trigger

  def run(character, %Action{id: :forward}) do
    Shell.info("You're walking cautiously and can see the next room.")
    {character, :forward}
  end
  def run(character, %Action{id: :search}) do
    healing = 5

    Shell.info("You search the room looking for something useful.")
    Shell.info("You find a treasure box with a healing potion inside.")
    Shell.info("You drink the potion and restore #{healing} hit points.")

    {
      DungeonCrawl.Character.heal(character, healing),
      :forward
    }
  end
end
```

The treasure trigger works like this: if the player tries to search the room, she'll find a healing potion. When the clause matches, the :search action will make the hero regain health. We use DungeonCrawl.Character.heal/2 to restore the hero's health.

We can create more challenging rooms. Let's create one where the enemy is hidden and attacks the hero first:

design_your_application/dungeon_crawl/lib/dungeon_crawl/room/triggers/enemy_hidden.ex

```
defmodule DungeonCrawl.Room.Triggers.EnemyHidden do
  alias DungeonCrawl.Room.Action
  alias Mix.Shell.IO, as: Shell

  @behaviour DungeonCrawl.Room.Trigger

  def run(character, %Action{id: :forward}) do
    Shell.info("You're walking cautiously and can see the next room.")
    {character, :forward}
  end
  def run(character, %Action{id: :rest}) do
    enemy = Enum.random(DungeonCrawl.Enemies.all)

    Shell.info("You search the room for a comfortable place to rest.")
    Shell.info("Suddenly...")
    Shell.info(enemy.description)
    Shell.info("The enemy #{enemy.name} surprises you and attacks first.")
```

```
      {_enemy, updated_char} = DungeonCrawl.Battle.fight(enemy, character)

      {
        updated_char,
        :forward
      }
    end
end
```

The hidden-enemy trigger works like this: if the player tries to rest in the room, an enemy will appear and start a battle. When the clause matches the rest action, it chooses a random enemy, invokes the fight/2 function, and makes the enemy attack first, passing the enemy in the first argument. That causes the enemy to attack first, making the hero always lose hit points and creating a challenging encounter.

We can create a similar trigger that instead will be good for the hero:

design_your_application/dungeon_crawl/lib/dungeon_crawl/room/triggers/rest.ex
```
defmodule DungeonCrawl.Room.Triggers.Rest do
  alias DungeonCrawl.Room.Action
  alias Mix.Shell.IO, as: Shell

  @behaviour DungeonCrawl.Room.Trigger

  def run(character, %Action{id: :forward}) do
    Shell.info("You're walking cautiously and can see the next room.")
    {character, :forward}
  end
  def run(character, %Action{id: :rest}) do
    healing = 3

    Shell.info("You search the room for a comfortable place to rest.")
    Shell.info("After a little rest you regain #{healing} hit points.")

    {
      DungeonCrawl.Character.heal(character, healing),
      :forward
    }
  end
end
```

The rest trigger works like this: if the player tries to relax in the room, she'll take a nap and have some hit points restored. When the clause matches, the rest action will make the hero restore health with the heal/2 function.

You can create even more triggers or combine them. For example, a trigger that makes the hero fight a boss battle before going to the exit, or a trigger that makes the player solve a puzzle. It's up to you to enhance the game with more challenges.

# Answers to Exercises

In this book, you'll find exercises from Chapter 2 through Chapter 5 to practice what you have learned. If you get stuck or you want to compare your answers, you can consult my answers here. The exercises of Chapters 6 and 7 were designed to be open-ended, which is why you won't find the answers here. Feel free to share your answers and discuss the exercises with other readers in this book's forum.[1]

## Answers for Chapter 2, Working with Variables and Functions

- You'll find how many dollars Sarah has spent by executing the following expression:

work_with_functions/answers/exercise_2.exs
```
(10 * 0.1) + (3 * 2) + 15
```

- You can show Bob's travel stats with the following code:

work_with_functions/answers/exercise_3.exs
```
distance = 200
hours = 4
velocity = distance / hours
IO.puts """
Travel distance: #{distance} km
Time: #{hours} hours
Average Velocity: #{velocity} km/h
"""
```

---

1.  https://forums.pragprog.com/forums/440

- The apply_tax function should be like this:

work_with_functions/answers/exercise_4.exs
```
apply_tax = fn price ->
  tax = price * 0.12
  IO.puts "Price: #{price + tax} - Tax: #{tax}"
end

Enum.each [12.5, 30.99, 250.49, 18.80], apply_tax
```

- Your MatchstickFactory should look like this:

work_with_functions/answers/exercise_5.ex
```
defmodule MatchstickFactory do
  @size_big 50
  @size_medium 20
  @size_small 5

  def boxes(matchsticks) do
    big_boxes = div(matchsticks, @size_big)
    remaining = rem(matchsticks, @size_big)

    medium_boxes = div(remaining, @size_medium)
    remaining = rem(remaining, @size_medium)

    small_boxes = div(remaining, @size_small)
    remaining = rem(remaining, @size_small)

    %{
      big: big_boxes,
      medium: medium_boxes,
      small: small_boxes,
      remaining_matchsticks: remaining
    }
  end
end
```

# Answers for Chapter 3, Using Pattern Matching to Control the Program Flow

- Here's the function that calculates the total points spent in attributes:

pattern_matching/answers/exercise_1.ex
```
defmodule CharacterAttributes do
  def total_spent(%{strength: str, dexterity: dex, intelligence: int}) do
    (str * 2) + (dex * 3) + (int * 3)
  end
end
```

- The Tic-Tac-Toe module should be like this:

pattern_matching/answers/exercise_2.ex

```elixir
defmodule TicTacToe do
  def winner({
    x, x, x,
    _, _, _,
    _, _, _
  }), do: {:winner, x}

  def winner({
    _, _, _,
    x, x, x,
    _, _, _
  }), do: {:winner, x}

  def winner({
    _, _, _,
    _, _, _,
    x, x, x
  }), do: {:winner, x}

  def winner({
    x, _, _,
    x, _, _,
    x, _, _
  }), do: {:winner, x}

  def winner({
    _, x, _,
    _, x, _,
    _, x, _
  }), do: {:winner, x}

  def winner({
    _, _, x,
    _, _, x,
    _, _, x
  }), do: {:winner, x}

  def winner({
    x, _, _,
    _, x, _,
    _, _, x
  }), do: {:winner, x}

  def winner({
    _, _, x,
    _, x, _,
    x, _, _
  }), do: {:winner, x}

  def winner(_board), do: :no_winner
end
```

- Here's how you can calculate the income tax of a salary:

pattern_matching/answers/exercise_3.ex
```
defmodule IncomeTax do
  def total(salary) when salary <= 2000, do: 0
  def total(salary) when salary <= 3000, do: salary * 0.05
  def total(salary) when salary <= 6000, do: salary * 0.1
  def total(salary), do: salary * 0.15
end
```

- Here's how a user can enter their salary and display their income tax and net wage:

pattern_matching/answers/exercise_4.exs
```
defmodule IncomeTax do
  def total(salary) when salary <= 2000, do: 0
  def total(salary) when salary <= 3000, do: salary * 0.05
  def total(salary) when salary <= 6000, do: salary * 0.1
  def total(salary), do: salary * 0.15
end

input =  IO.gets "Your salary:\n"

case Float.parse(input) do
 :error -> IO.puts "Invalid salary: #{input}"
 {salary, _} ->
   tax = IncomeTax.total(salary)
   IO.puts "Net wage: #{salary - tax} - Income tax: #{tax}"
end
```

# Answers for Chapter 4, Diving into Recursion

- Here's the code of how you can find the smallest and biggest numbers in a list:

recursion/answers/exercise_1.ex
```
defmodule MyList do
  def max([]), do: nil
  def max([a]), do: a
  def max([a, b | rest]) when a >= b, do: find_max(rest, a)
  def max([a, b | rest]) when a < b, do: find_max(rest, b)

  defp find_max([], max), do: max
  defp find_max([head | rest], max) when head >= max, do: find_max(rest, head)
  defp find_max([head | rest], max) when head < max, do: find_max(rest, max)

  def min([]), do: nil
  def min([a]), do: a
  def min([a, b | rest]) when a <= b, do: find_min(rest, a)
  def min([a, b | rest]) when a > b, do: find_min(rest, b)
```

```
  defp find_min([], min), do: min
    defp find_min([head | rest], min) when head <= min, do: find_min(rest, head)
    defp find_min([head | rest], min) when head > min, do: find_min(rest, min)
end
```

- You can filter magical items in the store using a function like this:

recursion/answers/exercise_2.ex
```
defmodule GeneralStore do
  def test_data do
    [
      %{title: "Longsword", price: 50, magic: false},
      %{title: "Healing Potion", price: 60, magic: true},
      %{title: "Rope", price: 10, magic: false},
      %{title: "Dragon's Spear", price: 100, magic: true},
    ]
  end

  def filter_items([], magic: magic), do: []
  def filter_items([item = %{magic: item_magic} | rest], magic: filter_magic)
      when item_magic == filter_magic do
    [item | filter_items(rest, magic: filter_magic)]
  end
  def filter_items([item | rest], magic: filter_magic) do
    filter_items(rest, magic: filter_magic)
  end
end
```

- Sort.descending/1 should look like this:

recursion/answers/exercise_3.ex
```
defmodule Sort do
  def descending([]), do: []
  def descending([a]), do: [a]
  def descending(list) do
    half_size = div(Enum.count(list), 2)
    {list_a, list_b} = Enum.split(list, half_size)
    merge(
      descending(list_a),
      descending(list_b)
    )
  end

  defp merge([], list_b), do: list_b
  defp merge(list_a, []), do: list_a
  defp merge([head_a | tail_a], list_b = [head_b | _]) when head_a >= head_b do
    [head_a | merge(tail_a, list_b)]
  end
  defp merge(list_a = [head_a | _], [head_b | tail_b]) when head_a < head_b do
    [head_b | merge(list_a, tail_b)]
  end
end
```

- Here's the tail-recursive version of the functions:

recursion/answers/exercise_4.ex
```elixir
defmodule Sum do
  def up_to(n), do: sum_up_to(n, 0)
  defp sum_up_to(0, sum), do: sum
  defp sum_up_to(n, sum), do: sum_up_to(n - 1, n + sum)
end

defmodule Math do
  def sum(list), do: sum_list(list, 0)
  defp sum_list([], sum), do: sum
  defp sum_list([head | tail], sum), do: sum_list(tail, head + sum)
end

defmodule Sort do
  def asc([]), do: []
  def asc([a]), do: [a]
  def asc(list) do
    half_size = div(Enum.count(list), 2)
    {list_a, list_b} = Enum.split(list, half_size)
    merge(
      asc(list_a),
      asc(list_b),
      []
    )
  end

  defp merge([], list_b, merged), do: merged ++ list_b
  defp merge(list_a, [], merged), do: merged ++ list_a
  defp merge([head_a | tail_a], list_b = [head_b | _], merged)
      when head_a <= head_b do
    merge(tail_a, list_b, merged ++ [head_a])
  end
  defp merge(list_a = [head_a | _], [head_b | tail_b], merged)
      when head_a > head_b do
    merge(list_a, tail_b, merged ++ [head_b])
  end
end
```

- The following code shows how the BreadthNavigator module should look:

recursion/answers/exercise_5.ex
```elixir
defmodule Navigator do
  @max_breadth 2

  def navigate(dir) do
    expanded_dir = Path.expand(dir)
    go_through([expanded_dir], 0)
  end

  defp go_through([], current_breadth), do: nil
  defp go_through(list, current_breadth) when current_breadth > @max_breadth,
      do: nil
```

```
  defp go_through([content | rest], current_breadth) do
    print_and_navigate(content, File.dir?(content))
    go_through(rest, current_breadth + 1)
  end

  defp print_and_navigate(_dir, false), do: nil
  defp print_and_navigate(dir, true) do
    IO.puts dir
    {:ok, children_dirs} = File.ls(dir)
    go_through(expand_dirs(children_dirs, dir), 0)
  end

  defp expand_dirs([], _relative_to), do: []
  defp expand_dirs([dir | dirs], relative_to) do
    expanded_dir = Path.expand(dir, relative_to)
    [expanded_dir | expand_dirs(dirs, relative_to)]
  end
end
```

# Answers for Chapter 5, Using Higher-Order Functions

- The EnchanterShop module should look like this:

higher_order_functions/answers/exercise_1.ex
```
defmodule EnchanterShop do
  def test_data do
    [
      %{title: "Longsword", price: 50, magic: false},
      %{title: "Healing Potion", price: 60, magic: true},
      %{title: "Rope", price: 10, magic: false},
      %{title: "Dragon's Spear", price: 100, magic: true},
    ]
  end
  @enchanter_name "Edwin"

  def enchant_for_sale(items) do
    Enum.map(items, &transform/1)
  end

  defp transform(item = %{magic: true}), do: item
  defp transform(item) do
    %{
      title: "#{@enchanter_name}'s #{item.title}",
      price: item.price * 3,
      magic: true
    }
  end
end
```

- Here's the Fibonacci sequence using streams:

higher_order_functions/answers/exercise_2.ex
```elixir
defmodule Fibonacci do
  def sequence(n) do
    Stream.unfold({0, 1}, fn {n1, n2} -> {n1, {n2, n1 + n2}} end)
    |> Enum.take(n)
  end
end
```

- Here's how you add the step of packing the screws:

higher_order_functions/answers/exercise_3.ex
```elixir
defmodule ScrewsFactory do
  def run(pieces) do
    pieces
    |> Stream.chunk(50)
    |> Stream.flat_map(&add_thread/1)
    |> Stream.chunk(100)
    |> Stream.flat_map(&add_head/1)
    |> Stream.chunk(30)
    |> Stream.flat_map(&pack/1)
    |> Enum.each(&output/1)
  end

  defp add_thread(pieces) do
    Process.sleep(50)
    Enum.map(pieces, &(&1 <> "--"))
  end

  defp add_head(pieces) do
    Process.sleep(100)
    Enum.map(pieces, &("o" <> &1))
  end

  defp pack(screws) do
    Process.sleep(70)
    Enum.map(screws, &("|" <> &1 <> "|"))
  end

  defp output(package) do
    IO.inspect(package)
  end
end
```

• The Quicksort should look like this:

higher_order_functions/answers/exercise_4.ex

```elixir
defmodule Quicksort do
  def sort([]), do: []
  def sort([pivot | tail]) do
    {lesser, greater} = Enum.split_with(tail, &(&1 <= pivot))
    sort(lesser) ++ [pivot] ++ sort(greater)
  end
end
```

# Bibliography

[Arm13]     Joe Armstrong. *Programming Erlang (2nd edition)*. The Pragmatic Bookshelf, Raleigh, NC, 2nd, 2013.

[Hal18]     Lance Halvorsen. *Functional Web Development with Elixir, OTP, and Phoenix*. The Pragmatic Bookshelf, Raleigh, NC, 2018.

[McC15]     Chris McCord. *Metaprogramming Elixir*. The Pragmatic Bookshelf, Raleigh, NC, 2015.

[Tho18]     Dave Thomas. *Programming Elixir ≥ 1.6*. The Pragmatic Bookshelf, Raleigh, NC, 2018.

[TV18]      Chris McCord, Bruce Tate and José Valim. *Programming Phoenix 1.3*. The Pragmatic Bookshelf, Raleigh, NC, 2018.

# Index

# Thank you!

How did you enjoy this book? Please let us know. Take a moment and email us at support@pragprog.com with your feedback. Tell us your story and you could win free ebooks. Please use the subject line "Book Feedback."

Ready for your next great Pragmatic Bookshelf book? Come on over to https://pragprog.com and use the coupon code BUYANOTHER2018 to save 30% on your next ebook.

Void where prohibited, restricted, or otherwise unwelcome. Do not use ebooks near water. If rash persists, see a doctor. Doesn't apply to *The Pragmatic Programmer* ebook because it's older than the Pragmatic Bookshelf itself. Side effects may include increased knowledge and skill, increased marketability, and deep satisfaction. Increase dosage regularly.

And thank you for your continued support,

Andy Hunt, Publisher

SAVE 30%!
Use coupon code
**BUYANOTHER2018**

# Learn Why, Then Learn How

Get started on your Elixir journey today.

## Adopting Elixir

Adoption is more than programming. Elixir is an exciting new language, but to successfully get your application from start to finish, you're going to need to know more than just the language. You need the case studies and strategies in this book. Learn the best practices for the whole life of your application, from design and team building, to managing stakeholders, to deployment and monitoring. Go beyond the syntax and the tools to learn the techniques you need to develop your Elixir application from concept to production.

Ben Marx, José Valim, Bruce Tate
(225 pages) ISBN: 9781680502527. $42.95
*https://pragprog.com/book/tvmelixir*

## Programming Elixir ≥ 1.6

This book is *the* introduction to Elixir for experienced programmers, completely updated for Elixir 1.6 and beyond. Explore functional programming without the academic overtones (tell me about monads just one more time). Create concurrent applications, but get them right without all the locking and consistency headaches. Meet Elixir, a modern, functional, concurrent language built on the rock-solid Erlang VM. Elixir's pragmatic syntax and built-in support for metaprogramming will make you productive and keep you interested for the long haul. Maybe the time is right for the Next Big Thing. Maybe it's Elixir.

Dave Thomas
(398 pages) ISBN: 9781680502992. $47.95
*https://pragprog.com/book/elixir16*

# A Better Web with Phoenix and Elm

Elixir and Phoenix on the server side with Elm on the front end gets you the best of both worlds in both worlds!

## Programming Phoenix 1.3

Don't accept the compromise between fast and beautiful: you can have it all. Phoenix creator Chris McCord, Elixir creator José Valim, and award-winning author Bruce Tate walk you through building an application that's fast and reliable. At every step, you'll learn from the Phoenix creators not just what to do, but why. Packed with insider insights and completely updated for Phoenix 1.3, this definitive guide will be your constant companion in your journey from Phoenix novice to expert, as you build the next generation of web applications.

Chris McCord, Bruce Tate and José Valim
(325 pages) ISBN: 9781680502268. $45.95
*https://pragprog.com/book/phoenix13*

## Programming Elm

Elm brings the safety and stability of functional programing to front-end development, making it one of the most popular new languages. Elm's functional nature and static typing means that run-time errors are nearly impossible, and it compiles to JavaScript for easy web deployment. This book helps you take advantage of this new language in your web site development. Learn how the Elm Architecture will help you create fast applications. Discover how to integrate Elm with JavaScript so you can update legacy applications. See how Elm tooling makes deployment quicker and easier.

Jeremy Fairbank
(250 pages) ISBN: 9781680502855. $40.95
*https://pragprog.com/book/jfelm*

# Dive Deep into OTP and Absinthe

Put it all together with Elixir, OTP, and Phoenix. Dive into GraphQL for better APIs in Elixir. It's all here.

## Functional Web Development with Elixir, OTP, and Phoenix

Elixir and Phoenix are generating tremendous excitement as an unbeatable platform for building modern web applications. For decades OTP has helped developers create incredibly robust, scalable applications with unparalleled uptime. Make the most of them as you build a stateful web app with Elixir, OTP, and Phoenix. Model domain entities without an ORM or a database. Manage server state and keep your code clean with OTP Behaviours. Layer on a Phoenix web interface without coupling it to the business logic. Open doors to powerful new techniques that will get you thinking about web development in fundamentally new ways.

Lance Halvorsen
(218 pages) ISBN: 9781680502435. $45.95
*https://pragprog.com/book/lhelph*

## Craft GraphQL APIs in Elixir with Absinthe

Your domain is rich and interconnected, and your API should be too. Upgrade your web API to GraphQL, leveraging its flexible queries to empower your users, and its declarative structure to simplify your code. Absinthe is the GraphQL toolkit for Elixir, a functional programming language designed to enable massive concurrency atop robust application architectures. Written by the creators of Absinthe, this book will help you take full advantage of these two groundbreaking technologies. Build your own flexible, high-performance APIs using step-by-step guidance and expert advice you won't find anywhere else.

Bruce Williams and Ben Wilson
(250 pages) ISBN: 9781680502558. $47.95
*https://pragprog.com/book/wwgraphql*

# The Pragmatic Bookshelf

The Pragmatic Bookshelf features books written by developers for developers. The titles continue the well-known Pragmatic Programmer style and continue to garner awards and rave reviews. As development gets more and more difficult, the Pragmatic Programmers will be there with more titles and products to help you stay on top of your game.

# Visit Us Online

### This Book's Home Page
*https://pragprog.com/book/cdc-elixir*
Source code from this book, errata, and other resources. Come give us feedback, too!

### Register for Updates
*https://pragprog.com/updates*
Be notified when updates and new books become available.

### Join the Community
*https://pragprog.com/community*
Read our weblogs, join our online discussions, participate in our mailing list, interact with our wiki, and benefit from the experience of other Pragmatic Programmers.

### New and Noteworthy
*https://pragprog.com/news*
Check out the latest pragmatic developments, new titles and other offerings.

# Save on the eBook

Save on the eBook versions of this title. Owning the paper version of this book entitles you to purchase the electronic versions at a terrific discount.

PDFs are great for carrying around on your laptop—they are hyperlinked, have color, and are fully searchable. Most titles are also available for the iPhone and iPod touch, Amazon Kindle, and other popular e-book readers.

Buy now at *https://pragprog.com/coupon*

# Contact Us

| | |
|---|---|
| Online Orders: | *https://pragprog.com/catalog* |
| Customer Service: | *support@pragprog.com* |
| International Rights: | *translations@pragprog.com* |
| Academic Use: | *academic@pragprog.com* |
| Write for Us: | *http://write-for-us.pragprog.com* |
| Or Call: | +1 800-699-7764 |